D0867879

The
Peter
Promise

Discovery House Publishers

Books, music, and videos that feed the soul with the Word of God

Box 3566 Grand Rapids, MI 49501

The Peter Promise

Powerful Principles from the Life of Peter

Luis Palau

with Ellen Bascuti

Discovery House Publishers is affiliated with RBC Ministries, Grand Rapids, Michigan 49512.

Discovery House books are distributed to the trade by Thomas Nelson Publishers, Nashville, Tennessee 37214.

Library of Congress Cataloging-in-Publication Data

Palau, Luis, 1934–
    [Walk on water, Pete!]
    The Peter promise / Luis Palau.
       p.   cm.
    Previously published: Portland, Or. : Multnomah Press, c1981.
    ISBN 1-57293-011-X
    1. Christian life. 2. Peter, the Apostle, Saint. I. Title.
BV4501.2.P27   1996
248.4—dc20   96-10501
                                          CIP

Printed in the United States of America

96 97 98 99 00 01 / CHG / 10 9 8 7 6 5 4 3 2

CONTENTS

DEDICATION

My special thanks to the late Mr. Fred Renich, whose messages and personal concern taught me to grow along with Peter.

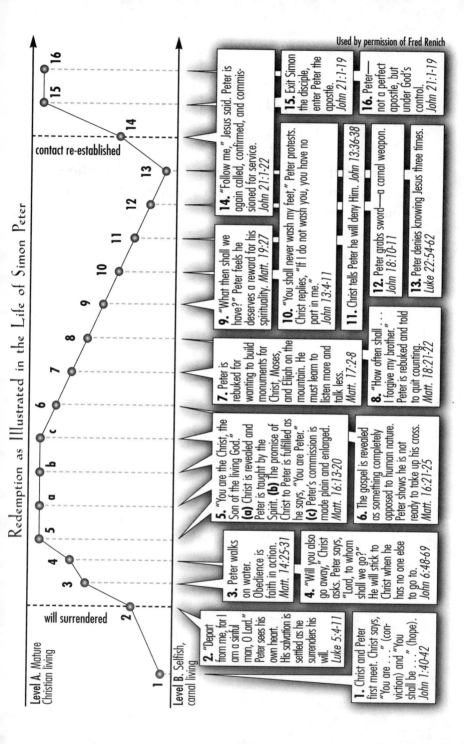

Redemption as Illustrated in the Life of Simon Peter

Used by permission of Fred Renich

INTRODUCTION

Many enthusiastic and zealous believers have asked me, "Luis, I want to serve God in a big way. I want to win souls to Christ, like you do. How did you get your big break to serve God through mass evangelistic crusades?"

There are no big breaks in crusade evangelism or any other kind of service for God. God leads in many small ways, and we learn obedience each time. As the saying goes, "Big doors turn on small hinges." God often uses insignificant events to bring great, far reaching changes.

I think the life of the apostle Peter demonstrates that principle quite clearly. When Jesus Christ entered Peter's life, his days as a fisherman ended and, through a series of events, he became a great apostle, the founding father of the church.

A similar change can happen to you. A small book, a little phrase, a brief encounter can change the whole course of a life.

Many years ago someone gave me a handbill advertising a meeting with a man named Dick Hillis, a "Prisoner of the Communists in China for two years."

The handbill also mentioned a Ray Stedman, pastor of Peninsula Bible Church in California. Because I had never met a Californian, I went to hear him. The message was good, and just to see what a Californian was like, I stayed afterward to meet Ray. He was suntanned, chubby, and nice.

Out of that simple encounter with two men, the whole course of my life was changed. Through Ray Stedman and Dr. Dick Hillis, God got me out of Argentina, directed me into Overseas Crusades, and later led me to form an evangelistic association. That one contact opened great doors for ministry, doors of opportunity God has given us.

If I had not met Ray, I would probably still be in Argentina ministering in a little assembly as if there were no other saints or sinners in the world.

How about you? You may feel uptight and limited in your experiences. You may feel crowded and hemmed in by life. I believe the Holy Spirit is waiting to open doors for you that are beyond your wildest dreams.

God is waiting to turn your life around with a word, an encounter, a seemingly insignificant event. Remember, "Big doors turn on small hinges." A little meeting, a short talk, maybe even this book could open up your whole future. That's my prayer.

I would love to hear from you, especially if you've been helped by reading this book. Please write to me at P.O. Box 1173, Portland, Oregon 97207.

Luis Palau

Chapter 1

SIMON, MEET PETER!

Not long ago I heard a woman make this statement: "I have never met a person changed by Jesus Christ."

What a shock to hear these words from a woman who has spent more than twelve years working in the church and in other Christian circles. I must say her statement shook me up. I don't know what expectations this woman has for Christians—they may be excessive. But her words made me think.

If the Christian life is all about the life-changing work of Jesus in our lives, then we should ask ourselves if we have been transformed.

Has there really been a change in my life, in your life, so that when Mrs. so-and-so looks at us she could say, "I have seen the power of God in that life. I know that person is a victorious Christian"?

I hope you are experiencing a victorious Christian life, but if you are anything like I was, you have spent many frustrating days sweating it out for God. You want to change, to become what He wants you to be. You give Him all you've got—reading the Bible more, praying more, witnessing more—but victory never seems to arrive. You feel defeated and are ready to throw in the towel.

It took me about eight years of zealously "doing" for God before I learned that it is not what you are doing for God, but rather what He wants to do in you and through you that counts (see Gal. 2:20).

That's the lesson Jesus Christ wants to teach every one of us. Jesus didn't save us to leave us where we are. He wants to change us from what we once were to what He wants us to be.

When Simon Peter met Jesus Christ, he did not realize what the future held for him. He was just a laborer, a poor man who fished by night and mended his nets by day—until the day he encountered Jesus Christ. He didn't even know who Jesus was. His brother Andrew brought him to Jesus. But the moment he met Christ, Simon the fisherman began a new life. This interesting incident is recorded in John 1:40–43:

> One of the two men who had heard what John said and had followed Jesus was Andrew, Simon Peter's brother. He went straight off and found his own brother, Simon, and told him, "We have found the Messiah!" (meaning, of course, Christ). And he brought him to Jesus.

Jesus looked steadily at him and said: "You are Simon, the son of John. From now on your name is Cephas" (that is, Peter, meaning "a rock").

Simon had never met the Lord Jesus. Yet the moment Simon came face to face with Him, the Lord told Simon his name, changed it to Peter, and made him a fantastic promise. Jesus told him, "By the time I'm through with you, Simon son of John, people are not going to call you Simon any more. Instead they are going to call you Peter, the rock."

What God is going to do in Peter's life serves as an excellent example of how God works His will. Through Peter we can watch God's redemption, His salvation, work itself out.

Redemption is characterized by three stages. First, there is redemption past. Second, redemption present. Finally, there is redemption future.

Redemption Past

Redemption past has been settled at the cross forever. Past redemption had to do with guilt and forgiveness of sins. When Christ died on the cross, He finished the work of redemption.

Some time ago one of my nephews, I'll call him Kenneth, was near death. He had AIDS, he was only twenty-five, and during a family reunion in the hills of northern California, Kenneth and I broke away for a short walk.

"Kenneth, you are going to die any day," I said. "Do you have eternal life?"

"Luis," Kenneth said, "I know God has forgiven me and I am going to heaven." For several years since his early teens, Kenneth had practiced homosexuality. More than that, in rebellion against God and his parents, he flaunted his lifestyle.

"Kenneth, how can you say that?" I replied. "You rebelled against God, you made fun of the Bible, you hurt your family, and now you say you've got eternal life . . . just like that?"

Kenneth looked at me straight in the eye, and he said, "Luis, when the doctor said I had AIDS I realized what a fool I had been. I repented of my sins, and I know God has had mercy on me."

Several short months later in excruciating physical pain, Kenneth went to be with the Lord. My nephew did not deserve God's grace. I didn't either. None of us do, but God's words leave no doubt: "In [Jesus] we have redemption through his blood, the forgiveness of [our] sins" (Eph. 1:7, NIV).

That redemption, that forgiveness is final and is freely available to everyone who accepts Christ. Redemption past guarantees that as a man or woman, boy or girl, your sins are forgiven and all washed away. It guarantees that everything in your past, all the nitty-gritty, all the hanky-panky, all that is condemning is forgiven and washed away through the blood of Christ on the cross.

What a great feeling it is to begin life anew after salvation. That is redemption past and it is available through the blood at the cross. I hope all of you have experienced that forgiveness, that redemption.

Redemption Future

Redemption future occurs when the Lord gives us a total experience of Himself. He is going to take us out of this place of sin, this world, and make us perfect forever.

My father died when I was ten years old. And my mother, at age eighty-three, departed this earth. Although their deaths caused me great pain, I know both my parents went to heaven and entered the presence of the Lord.

That's the hope of redemption future. One day, at the resurrection, our bodies will rise from the dead and be joined with our spirits. The Bible says in 1 Corinthians 15 that we will receive a spiritual and eternal body. We will be perfect!

When we are perfect, there will be no more problems, no more suffering, no more rebellion, no more temptations, no more anything that drags us down and destroys us. Sin will be no more! Future redemption will be final redemption.

Redemption Now

Redemption now is the immediate concern of all believers. Through redemption now we learn that God wants to change us from self-centered men and women into mature, Spirit-controlled vessels. He wants to free us from the tyranny of selfishness that tends to make us ego-centered, proud, haughty people whom God cannot use to work His will.

As we look at the life of Peter and the things that happened to him, we will see how God works out redemption now, and we can learn from it.

Peter's redemption experience can be applied to the lives of young people who question God's will for their future; to the elderly who feel, perhaps, that they can no longer serve God at their age; to the middle-aged who may have failed God and feel like giving up.

We all are going to see ourselves in the life of Peter. As we get to know Peter we will find that he is just like every one of us. He possesses all the faults and frailties we wish did not exist in us.

For that reason, studying the life of Peter might make some people very uncomfortable—and might frighten others. But the rewards of watching God work are so thrilling that Peter's life greatly blesses those who watch and learn.

Sincere Hypocrites

When I was a young Christian I sincerely wanted to be rid of obstacles to growth. But I didn't know how to do it. So after a few months of trying and failing, I became a marvelous actor.

I knew it was a big put-on. But it was a sincere put-on. Christians were supposed to be happy. Since I wanted desperately to be a good Christian, I pretended to have great joy even when I was miserable. Perhaps I thought if I pretended hard enough the pretense would come true. Unfortunately, it doesn't work that way.

I became such a good actor that mothers would come up to me and say, "Oh, Luis, if only my son Charlie were like you! I would be so thrilled if he were as dedicated and as holy as you are."

I'd tell them, "Madam, if you only knew my heart, you wouldn't want Charlie to be like me."

And Charlie's mother would say, "Oh, and you're so humble on top of it all!"

I had managed, in my great effort to be a sincere Christian, to impress others to such a degree that they believed my charade. They thought I was something that inside I knew I wasn't.

Many Christians are, at best, sincere hypocrites. Although people often believe that hypocrisy is the worst possible vice for a Christian to have, many of those same people are sincere hypocrites. If the truth were known, each of us at one time or another has been a sincere hypocrite, even Peter.

Peter didn't know the secret of a happy life, but he sure made a good impression because of his smoke screen of self-confidence. As we pursue our study of Peter, we will discover that Peter was in many ways the most impressive of all the disciples. Yet he was one who needed to learn the most dramatic lessons.

THE FIRST STEP
God Works Out Redemption Now

Notice two things about Peter's initial encounter with Jesus. First, the Lord looked at him as the old man, unredeemed, and *He called him by his old name, Simon.*

Simon was an interesting character. He was an aggressive, boastful, self-confident, loud-mouthed, impulsive man. Just imagine him when his brother brought him to Jesus. Simon came, possibly, with a swagger and a cynical look, thinking, "Who in the world can this man be to cause my brother to be so interested in introducing me?"

The Lord Jesus looked at Simon and, of course, knew all he was thinking. Imagine what a sobering experience it must have been for a man like Simon to have Jesus so quickly and simply tell him who he was.

Jesus said, "You are Simon, the son of John." With that, Jesus cut through all the details of his life, all the qualities that made up the character of Simon and, with a name, described the natural man, the old man.

Christ was saying vastly more than it might seem on the surface. He was saying, "Simon, I know you. You are yet unrepentant and unredeemed, but before I'm through with you, you will have come all the way to Me flat on your face in humility. I will teach you to know yourself as I know you."

Future Promise

But Jesus didn't stop with a description of the natural man. A second thing happened when Simon encountered Jesus. Jesus went on to say, *"You shall be called Peter, the rock."*

Jesus could look at him and say to him, "Simon, listen to Me. I know all the skeletons in your closet, every one of them. If I were to open you up and let people see inside, you would run away in fear and mortification. But, Simon, I love you. And because I love you, I'm going to take hold of you. By the time

I'm through with you, I'm going to redeem you, I'm going to control you, I'm going to mold you so much that your character and your life are going to be completely different. You will be so altered by the time I'm through with you, Simon, that we'll have to change your name. You will be called Peter because you will be a rock to help other people."

With the dynamic of Christ behind that promise, Simon didn't stand a chance. He was completely transformed. What Jesus promised, happened. And if it happened to Simon, it can happen to anyone open to Christ.

Simon had all the weaknesses, all the sins that you and I struggle with. Yet by the time Jesus Christ was through He made Simon the great apostle Peter.

The basis of our hope is found in Jesus' promise to Simon: "You shall be . . ." (RSV). The Lord didn't say, "Maybe, Simon. Perhaps, if you're good, Simon." He said, "You *shall* be a rock."

Philippians 1:6 says, "I feel sure that the one who has begun his good work in you will go on developing it until the day of Jesus Christ."

When God takes a person in hand, no matter how wild a character he or she may be, life change results. God makes us what we ought to be.

When Jesus changed Simon's name, He was looking several years ahead. At that time Peter was a long way from being a rock, but Jesus knew there would come a time when Peter and a handful of others would turn the world upside down with their faith and power.

Maturing Process

A few years ago, Ernie Horn was involved in the planning for our crusade in Fort Worth when a tragic event changed his life. A young policeman friend of his was killed, shot by a gang member in a Fort Worth park.

A few days after his friend's funeral, Ernie, owner of E. Horn Construction, was at a weekly prayer meeting for the upcoming crusade when the Lord spoke to his heart, saying, "If I can't send My people to be part of the solution, who am I going to send?"

The Lord used Ernie to mobilize community and denominational leaders to work at solving problems in the inner city. But first he dealt with Ernie's heart, exposing a dark side: racial prejudice. It showed up most overtly at work. Ernie had just hired additional iron workers—all white—for a construction project. Every interview with a black man concluded the same way: "We'll get back with you later."

As Ernie says, "If God was fixin' to do a new thing, I had to get out of His way and let Him do it."

Ernie and crusade leaders in Fort Worth called a meeting of some thirty black pastors. Ernie's idea was to enlist their support for a youth rally in an inner-city park.

Sitting in a circle face to face with mostly black people, Ernie fought back tears, gripped by conviction. As he looked in their eyes, Ernie confessed his prejudice and sin, and how in his construction business he had acted with partiality. He repented and asked for forgiveness.

With only a few days' notice, four thousand young people—including rival gang members—showed up for a "reconciliation rally" at a Fort Worth park.

Then, spearheaded by Ernie, volunteers canvassed inner-city neighborhoods, inviting young people to the crusade. Buses brought more than five hundred young people to the Convention Center. On the crusade's youth night, the crowd of nine thousand erupted in applause as three inner-city gang members were the first to make their way to the area in front of the platform to profess their newfound faith in Christ.

God has promised to bring us to maturity but, as Ernie learned, we must get out of God's way and let Him work in us.

All of us when we receive Jesus Christ are just spiritual babies. But once Christ begins His work in us, we begin to grow from babyhood into spiritual adolescence, and then into maturity in Jesus Christ because Christ is at work in our hearts.

In 1 Thessalonians 5:24 we are promised, "He who calls you is utterly faithful and he will finish what he has set out to do." God promises to do His work of redemption now in us; He *will* bring us to maturity.

You may say to yourself, "If you knew me, you wouldn't be so positive. Nobody can handle me. I have such rotten passions, such a twisted mind that I can't straighten myself out."

You are right. You can't make yourself into the person you ought to be. But if you let Jesus Christ who indwells you take over, He will do it for you. Jesus has given us His word.

Have you heard the voice of Jesus Christ as Simon did? What has God promised you? He knows you as He knew Simon, and He can change you as He did Simon. He wants to do something with you, to turn the world upside down through you.

God can change you whether you are young or old, rich or poor. If God has spoken to you, then you can expect Him to do what He has promised to do. You can expect Him to turn you around and change your name.

Chapter 2

START WALKING
ON WATER

God loves to work through people to change the world. I realized this truth once again during our evangelistic Easter festival in Kathmandu, Nepal.

For centuries this remote country, hidden in the Himalayas between India and China, had almost no gospel witness. In 1960 there were only twenty-five baptized Christians. Since the revolution of 1990, which brought democracy and religious freedom to Nepal, the size of the church has increased to around 150,000.

People can trace the coming of the gospel to Nepal back to a few men and women. One Nepalese man shared Jesus Christ with those coming and going over the border in the days when the government prohibited evangelization.

He would approach the people who had gotten off the train from India and talk to them about Jesus while they were waiting for a cattle-drawn cart to take them to Nepal.

Slowly but surely, a growing number of men and women began to believe in Jesus, to receive Him as Savior. I discovered that many of the Christian leaders in Nepal today are the fruit of this man's labor.

The Lord loves to work through people, but He can only work through people who are willing to be changed. People like Simon Peter and people like you and me can be used by God to do amazing things. Before the Lord can really work through us, however, He has to polish us.

That's what we learned from Peter's first encounter with Jesus Christ in John 1:42. The Lord knew all about Peter and the skeletons in his closet. But Jesus promised to change Peter, to bring him to maturity, and to use him in a great way.

God can use us from the moment we become believers. But we all have many undesirable attitudes and habits that He simply must change before He can use us in an extraordinary way.

Born to Grow

After his coach told him what Jesus did for him on the cross, Eugene Robinson, professional football player for the Seattle Seahawks, trusted Jesus Christ as his Savior.

Immediately Eugene asked, "Coach, teach me the fundamentals of Christianity."

Eugene knew the importance of learning the basics. In any sport, the fundamentals are essential if you want a winning sports career. A player must learn how to hit, catch, kick, or throw the ball and know the rules of the game to perform successfully.

The same is true in Christianity. We are born into God's family as spiritual babies, and we must learn and develop and grow if we are to become victorious Christians.

Sadly, many Christians go through life as babes in Christ. Unless they learn the fundamentals and allow the indwelling Christ to raise them to maturity, they will forever be spiritual babies.

You and I both know Christians who are spiritual babies. Humanly speaking they may be forty, sixty, even eighty years old, but spiritually speaking they continue to behave like children in the church and at home. They still have temper tantrums: they throw things, they give people the silent treatment, they yell and scream when things don't go the way they want.

We all begin the Christian life as spiritual babies, and there's nothing wrong with that. God doesn't expect us to be immediate spiritual giants of the faith. Maturity is a process.

Peter himself went from spiritual immaturity to spiritual maturity. Peter first encountered Jesus Christ as a spiritual baby, then experienced Him as a growing believer, and finally conducted himself as a Spirit-filled apostle.

Peter stumbled and faltered along the way, as all growing Christians will, but by God's grace he recovered and continued his walk to perfect maturity.

THE SECOND STEP
God Controls Circumstances of Life

I talked with a twenty-year-old college student who told me a familiar story. "The thing that bothers me," he confessed, "is that I've received Christ as my Savior, but I have all the same problems I had before. I don't have victory. When I ask Christians what the solution is, I'm told to read the Bible more and pray more and witness more. I've been doing that faithfully and haven't yet found the secret of real victory. It seems all I do is struggle, struggle, struggle. It isn't a pleasant experience. Jesus Christ is my Savior, but I don't feel He's real to me. I want to feel that He's alive to me, that He's right here controlling and directing me as I try to walk with God."

This was also Peter's experience. He didn't understand that Jesus could control and direct his life until God intervened. God often needs to waken us, like Peter, by some dramatic experience before we will face the fact that Jesus Christ can be a reality in our lives.

In Luke 5:4–11, Peter takes a second step toward maturity, a step I call providence, or circumstances of life controlled by God.

When [Jesus] had finished speaking, he said to Simon, "Push out now into deep water and let down your nets for a catch."

Simon replied, "Master! We've worked all night and never caught a thing, but if you say so I'll let the nets down."

And when they had done this, they caught an enormous shoal of fish—so big that the nets began to tear. So they signaled to their friends in the other boat to come and help them. They came and filled both the boats to sinking point. When Simon Peter saw this, he fell on his knees before Jesus and said, "Keep away from me, Lord, for I'm only a sinful man!"

For he and his companions (including Zebedee's sons, James and John, Simon's partners) were staggered at the haul of fish that they had made.

Jesus said to Simon: "Don't be afraid, Simon. From now on your catch will be *men*."

So they brought the boats ashore, left everything and followed him.

Brokenness of Heart

In his second meeting with Christ, *Peter saw something of his own heart.* After they had caught so many fish, Peter fell at the feet of Jesus and said, "Keep away from me, Lord, for I'm only a sinful man!" (Luke 5:8). Peter realized he wasn't worthy to meet Jesus as he now saw himself. He had initially doubted when Jesus said to let down the nets, but when he saw the miracle of the fish, his honest heart compelled him to fall to his knees in submission.

We must individually come to the place where we discover our own real sinfulness of heart. After an evangelistic meeting in Spokane, Washington, a twelve-year-old boy asked me, "Mr. Palau, do you think God could forgive a rotten sinner?" He went on to tell me how he would sneak out of his house at night to engage in homosexual acts with a buddy of his. His mom didn't know where her boy was going or what he was doing. He was convinced God could never forgive him and the thought broke his heart.

This boy had faced up to his sinfulness and need for salvation. He had no illusions of his goodness. That's the position at which every person must arrive.

True Christians have faced their need for salvation and have asked for forgiveness. However, many more people have not. They refuse to face the wickedness and evil of their own hearts and resent it when told that they are sinners and evil.

I'm reminded of a young man in Alaska who is serving time in prison. He was seventeen and drunk when he ran a red light and killed two young women. Surely this is a person who would welcome an offer of forgiveness. Probably not. He is suing the liquor store that sold him the booze. The lawsuit demands compensation for the financial losses he suffered as a result of his imprisonment and for his emotional pain.

Someone who hasn't discovered what Peter discovered cannot go very far with God. Until we realize our wickedness, our malice, the corruption of our hearts, we can never find God in a living and real way.

As long as we continue to believe that we are all right, that we are not all that bad, as long as we think we can make it on our own, we are lost. But the moment we fall on our faces in humility and ask Him for forgiveness, He *will* forgive—no matter how evil or corrupt we are.

Like Peter, we must come to the point where we realize our lostness. When we experience brokenness of heart and feel God can never forgive us, that is when God can work.

Confirmation of Call

Not only did Peter see something of his own heart in this second meeting with Christ, *he also saw something of what God is going to do in him.* In verse 10 Jesus says, "Don't be afraid, Simon. From now on your catch will be *men*."

The first time the Lord encountered Simon, He gave him a general overview. "I'm going to deal with you, Simon. You shall be Peter, a rock." The second time, He began to clarify His mission in Peter's life. "Don't be afraid, Peter, from now on you are going to catch men." He began to specify a little more of what He was prepared to do with Peter's life.

When Christ takes over our lives, He promises to forgive us, to bless us, and to make us into mature men and women. Then, slowly, He begins to point out and clarify what He is going to do with our lives.

I remember when I was seventeen listening to a shortwave HCJB radio program broadcast from Quito, Ecuador. I didn't hear the preacher's name, but I heard him calling men to come to Jesus Christ in a vibrant, somewhat high-pitched, and excited voice. The whole program left me exhilarated. Later I realized I had been listening to Billy Graham.

Stretched out on that living-room floor, I prayed: "Jesus, someday use me on the radio to bring others to You, just as this program has firmed up my resolve to completely live for You."

Little did I know that one day I would preach to tens of millions of people over hundreds of Christian radio networks and stations here in America and around the world. God gave me a glimpse of His plan for my life.

Peter was on his knees, thinking that Christ was going to reject him because he faced his own sinfulness, and instead Christ reconfirmed Peter's call. The first time, Jesus gave Peter a promise. The second time, Jesus gave him a plan.

Surrender of Will

The encounter with Jesus results in a third response by Peter. *He responded with full surrender of his will.* In verse 11 Peter does a wonderful thing that many Christians have done since. "So they pulled their boats up on shore, left everything and followed him" (NIV).

While Jim Montgomery was a missionary in the Philippines, he envisioned a tremendous plan he called DAWN—Disciple A Whole Nation. His idea was to establish churches within walking distance of every person in that nation.

He wrote many prayer letters, but no one would support his new venture because it sounded too big, too idealistic. Jim, however, wouldn't give up. The idea of DAWN burned in his soul.

Jim came back to the U.S., sold his house—the one security he had—and funded the beginning of the DAWN program. When I heard what he had done, I thought, *The Lord's going to honor Jim.* And He has. The DAWN program has spread to Africa, Latin America, Asia, and Europe. Jim started out sacrificing quietly for the cause of Jesus Christ, and God used him in a mighty way.

Today, you may have a burning fire in your heart to win people to Jesus Christ. You may have a plan or a program you know God could use for His glory. If God truly is speaking to you, step out in faith and obey Him.

When God calls you, it does not necessarily mean you have to sell everything and give away all your money. God may call you to keep your business.

In John 21:3, we are told that Peter went back to his boats. How could he have gone back to his trade if he had given them all up three years before?

Obedience to God's call does not automatically require material poverty. The important thing is fully committing your heart and spirit when Jesus speaks to you. Peter had this type of commitment. Somebody else would have to care for the boats and nets in the interval. His business could wait; Jesus Christ could not!

Partnership with God

Three important things have happened to Peter, but he is about to learn a fourth thing: the *fruitfulness of divine partnership.*

In Luke 5:5–7, Jesus recognizes Peter's gifts and acknowledges his abilities. He says, in effect, "You're a good fisherman, Peter, but if you and I start working as one, there is no limit to what God can do through your life. Unlimited fruitfulness can take place in your life."

This is a big lesson for any Christian to learn. Most of us are brought up with the idea that when we receive Christ all that remains is to roll up our sleeves and sweat it out for the Lord.

After I spoke at a conference about the divine partnership we can have in Jesus, an elderly missionary gentleman told me, "Luis, I have been on the field for more than forty years. I have worked for God as hard as I could, but it's brought little but frustration. Now I see why. Until today, I don't think I have ever really known what it meant to allow the risen Christ to do the living in me."

Many sincere people commit themselves to serving Christ with all their being. Often during an emotional moment or at a dynamic service, they promise faithfulness, consecration, dedication, devotion, and love. But a few months or even years later, they are like deflated balloons. The Christian commitment that was growing so big and looked so beautiful and full suddenly became flat and limp.

Why? Because they have not yet learned what God taught Peter and is trying to teach every man and woman: We cannot do it alone. John 15:5 says, "I am the vine; you are the branches. If a man remains in me and I in him, he will bear much fruit" (NIV).

Those with a good education, a good Christian background, and knowledge of the Bible find this truth especially difficult to fathom. They believe that memorizing verse upon verse of the Bible, studying the books of well-known theologians, and dedicating themselves to the church are all that's needed to have fruitful and fulfilling Christian lives.

Controlled by the Holy Spirit

Many years passed before I learned to rely on the power of the indwelling Christ. I received Christ when I was twelve years old. During those first few years I was a typical convert. Although my spiritual mentor was a great soul winner, he was a weak spiritual bodybuilder. He insisted that just reading, praying, and witnessing was all I needed to grow.

It wasn't, of course. I cooled off quickly. When I was seventeen, the Lord spoke to my heart in a marvelous way, took me out of the foolishness of the world, and brought me back to Him. I was baptized and bought myself a new Bible. I discovered a strong, new self-confidence.

I began to teach a Sunday school class, to hold a Bible study in my garage, and to preach on street corners. I was convinced if I was dedicated enough, God would use me to do great things.

But during those years from seventeen to twenty-five, I had an experience that dragged me down. A group of young fellows and I worked together in our church. We loved the Lord, but we experienced so many ups and downs that we eventually got tired. I began to get discouraged and say to myself, "How long are things going to go on like this? When am I going to finally make it? When do I finally arrive?"

The turning point in my Christian life came during one chapel service at graduate school. As I listened to the sermon, I realized I could do nothing for God. Everything in my ministry was worthless unless God was in it. Only He could make it work.

Galatians 2:20 brought it all together for me: "I have been crucified with Christ; it is no longer I who live, but Christ who lives in me; and the life I now live in the flesh I live by faith in the Son of God, who loved me and gave himself for me" (RSV).

The secret here is "not I, but Christ" in me. It's not what we are going to do for Him but rather what He is going to do through us. It's His power that controls our dispositions, enables us to serve, and corrects and directs us.

We'll still make mistakes. God doesn't take away the temptations or exempt us from failures. He simply assures us He has covered it all, and He gives us the power for future victories.

It took me eight long years to learn the biggest lesson God wants to teach us. Why do we refuse His teaching for so long? I think it's because we are impatient and arrogant. We don't like the idea that somehow we don't have what it takes.

Although we may not say so openly, many of us who sincerely love Christ think we've got it made. We secretly say, "You're going to see what I can do. Oh, boy, is the Lord going to be proud of me."

Peter provides us with an excellent example of someone who believed this misconception. At this point in Peter's life, his salvation became settled. His will was surrendered. First *the Lord called him.* Then *he actually became sure of his salvation.* Christ put His hand on Peter and promised him a life of fishing for men. Peter, at this point, left everything and followed the Lord Jesus. He's in. He's made it.

But receiving Christ is only crossing the line. All that Peter had experienced so far was just the beginning. When you receive Christ your sins are forgiven and washed away. Redemption is taken care of. Your past is forgotten and all the skeletons in your closet are buried at the Cross. No longer do you need to worry about your relationship with God. You've been redeemed.

After salvation comes the business of daily living, and that is where most of us fail. Thousands, perhaps millions, of true Christians, real children of God, get stuck right here. For thirty or forty years they stay where they are, never getting beyond this point. They're happy they're saved, they know they're going to heaven, but there's no growth here on earth.

Having to function as Christians, having to operate as believers every day, having to walk the walk and talk the talk is where many fail. It's a pitiful sight.

But, Peter did *not* stop growing and learning. After the Lord called him, and after Peter actually became sure of his salvation, then Peter took yet another step.

THE THIRD STEP
God Directs in Obedience of Faith

I once attended a dinner in Colombia, South America, aimed at praying for the nation. For the first time in the history of Colombia, the president, his cabinet, and the senate attended an event hosted by evangelicals.

During the meal, the president of Colombia said to me, "You know, Palau, the reason I'm here tonight is because of Jimmy Carter." He went on to explain that when all the leaders of Latin America gathered to sign the Panama Canal treaty, President Jimmy Carter invited every leader—right- and left-wing radicals, conservatives and liberals, republicans and democrats—to a Bible study at the White House.

The next morning at the study, Carter asked each of the men to read a verse of Matthew 24. Carter then explained what he thought it meant when Jesus spoke of wars, pestilence, and darkness. Then Carter closed in prayer.

"Palau," the president of Colombia said to me, "I was truly impressed that Carter cared that much for us. It isn't diplomatic to speak freely about spiritual things, but I realized that Carter really liked us and wanted us to know Jesus Christ."

When President Carter invited those men to a Bible study, he never knew the result. He never knew what doors it would open. He just obeyed the Spirit's prompting.

If we are to continue to grow, we must learn to obey God's Word no matter what. *Obedience of faith* to the Word is what Peter learned in his next encounter with Jesus.

In Matthew 14:25–31, we read,

> In the small hours Jesus went out to them, walking on the water of the lake. When the disciples caught sight of him walking on the water they were terrified. "It's a ghost!" they said, and screamed with fear.
>
> But at once Jesus spoke to them, "It's all right! It's I myself, don't be afraid!"
>
> "Lord, if it's really you," said Peter, "tell me to come to you on the water."
>
> "Come on, then," replied Jesus.
>
> Peter stepped down from the boat and did walk on the water, making for Jesus. But when he saw the fury of the wind he panicked and began to sink, calling out, "Lord save me!"
>
> At once Jesus reached out his hand and caught him, saying, "You little-faith! What made you lose your nerve like that?"

In the middle of high winds and rolling waves, Peter dared to step out of a tossing fishing boat onto the water, believing that the figure coming toward them was his Master. Peter was looking for excitement when he said, "Lord, let me come."

What an outrageous thing to do, and yet the Lord Jesus said, "Come ahead! I have a lesson to teach you." The Lord delights in teaching lessons to His children.

Test of Faith

Isn't it great to know Jesus Christ loves us and can teach us humility, faith, and trust in spite of our conceit and arrogance? Yet He is gracious and teaches us in a loving way. He doesn't push us too much, although He sometimes lets us corner ourselves. When that happens, all we need to do is call, "Lord, help me!" and He will immediately reach out His hand and catch us.

When Peter obeyed Jesus Christ's call to walk on the water, Peter walked on the water. Peter put his faith into action and obeyed. Obedience is faith in action.

Few Christians get to test their obedience and faith in such dramatic ways. Sadly, too few Christians dare or bother to test their faith in any way at all.

Many people who claim they follow Jesus Christ and do extreme things in their own strength actually dishonor Jesus Christ. A fanatic walks on his own steam. Eventually his pretense will fail him and he will begin to struggle and sink. Peter, however, walked on God's command. There is a vast difference between the two.

Walk on Water

One snowy January I was scheduled to preach at a church in New York. Before the meeting started, a distinguished-looking gentleman with a cane entered the sanctuary, walked to the front of the church, introduced himself and asked to speak with me after the service. We arranged to meet at the home of the family with whom I was staying.

In the car on the way to their house, my hosts told me about the gentleman with the cane. "Now Luis," they said, "you need to know that this gentleman is one of the most distinguished ophthalmologists in the country. His textbooks are studied in many of the major universities. He's been away from the Lord since we were in university together, but something has been on his heart during the last few weeks."

At the house my hosts excused themselves so the doctor and I could talk privately for a few minutes.

"Young man," he said, "I have a question to ask you, and based on the answer you give me, I'm going to make a big decision.

"I'm an ophthalmologist. I've made a lot of money. I'm well respected. Most people think I'm a success. But my daughter has no interest in God and my son is going to hell because I've never shared the gospel with him. For years I've questioned how I've spent my entire adult life."

Then he explained further. "When I was in university, some forty-two years ago, a missionary by the name of John R. Mott came and spoke about the need in the Middle East for ophthalmologists to help treat eye diseases, and I felt the call of God. When he gave the invitation, I made a commitment to go and serve Jesus Christ on the mission field. I made a commitment to use my medical skills for God's glory.

"But when graduation came, I married and my friends and relatives began to warn me about the dangers of living in the Middle East, about the sacrifices a missionary must make, about foolishly wasting my education. They said, 'Don't do it.' The pride of life got a hold of me, I turned down the Lord's call, and I never did go to the mission field. Instead, I started my own practice here in the States."

Then he added, "And I want you to know, I haven't had one day of peace in forty-two years. Now I'm retired and I've asked my wife to go with me to Afghanistan so we can finish our last days serving the Lord in mission work. I've said, 'Let's at least obey God at the end of our lives.' But she doesn't want to go, so tell me, shall I go or shall I stay?"

In typical Latin fashion, I put my arm around him and said, "Brother, I believe you should go."

He began to cry. "Thank you! I will go. God's been calling me for forty-two years. This time no one is going to stop me."

Six months later a friend of mine told me the doctor was in Afghanistan with his wife. "Even though he's in bad health, Dr. Jones is like a teenager all over again; he is so excited."

I saw the doctor again several months later. He told me, "Thank you, Luis, for telling me I should go to Afghanistan. I have redeemed those forty-two years I lost in just one year." About two months later he went to be with the Lord.

God longs to teach us how to start walking on water. He encourages us to start stepping out by faith. Like the elderly doctor, dare to step out and do whatever God has said to you.

God may have spoken to you ten years ago. He may be speaking to you now with no response. In the back of your mind the Holy Spirit keeps pleading with you to obey the Word of God that He spoke to you so many years ago.

If God faithfully reminds you that He spoke to you sometime, somewhere about something, find the courage to step out by faith on the Word of Jesus Christ. Lack of courage results in a dull, unhappy, unfruitful, and discouraged life. If you dare to step out, you will enjoy life and begin to walk in the fullness of the Spirit. It is never too late to respond to Him.

Abraham's Example

Every Christian ought to learn to walk on water. All through the Bible, God calls His chosen "men of faith." What does that mean? Simply that they acted with courage, the type of courage Peter displayed when he walked on the water.

Abraham was one of these great men of faith. He didn't walk on water, but he walked on desert sand at God's command. Hebrews 11:8 tells us, "By faith Abraham, when called to go to a place he would later receive as his inheritance, obeyed and went, even though he did not know where he was going" (NIV).

When God called Abraham, he had no idea where God was taking him. Imagine the faith it took to believe God and step out. All Abraham had was God's statement, "I'm going to give you a land for your descendants. And they will number more than the stars in the sky or the grains of sand on the shore. Come with me and I will take you to this land." It was enough for Abraham to know it was God who spoke, and he began moving by faith in the will of God. Abraham's obedience was faith in action.

Any believer can have the same experience when he or she begins to walk by faith in the indwelling Holy Spirit. Once we obey the Lord and step out in faith, we will be able to do anything, because all things are possible to those who believe.

Impossible as it seemed, Peter believed he would walk to Jesus on the water and stepped out in faith toward Christ. When Peter got near Jesus, he suddenly took his eyes off Him and immediately began to sink. But when he cried, "Lord, help me!" Jesus stretched out His hand, picked him up and said, "Why did you doubt, man of small faith?"

It is entirely possible, human nature being what it is, that at the moment Peter stood on the heaving water, looked back at the men in the boat, and considered that very few people had ever stood on water, he exclaimed, "Hey, look at me. I'm standing on water!" Christ had been forgotten and Peter was exulting in the accomplishment.

Power from God

So many of us forget where the power in our lives comes from. We have a spiritual experience, receive an answer to prayer, or win a soul to Jesus Christ and at that moment of glory and excitement, we suddenly forget that it was the power of God at work in and through us. The moment we become self-confident, down we go.

It must have hurt Peter when the Lord asked him where his faith had gone. After all, he *had* stepped out of the boat onto the waves. He *had* walked on water all the way to Christ. And yet Christ told him he was lacking in faith.

God *expects* us to obey so He can show us His power, and we are often surprised by how great He is. Little things for God seem so momentous to us.

I remember the first time God answered one of my prayers. It was such a simple request that I almost hesitate to tell about it.

While living in Argentina, I worked in a bank. At this particular time, the bank had been on strike for forty-two days, the banking system was in absolute shambles, and of course, no salaries were being paid. My mother, a widow, was caring for my five sisters and one brother using what I earned, but we had absolutely run out of money.

After reading a book about the experiences of George Müller, a great man of faith, I said, "Lord, I have never actually experienced for myself a true answer to prayer. I wish You would show me one answer to prayer. Send me some money so I can take the bus to the bank. Send it to me in some way that indicates the money came from You."

My mother was a woman of great faith, and I'd seen God answer many of her prayers. But I wanted an answer for myself.

The next morning I got up early since the bank opened at 7:00 in the summer. I had already planned how the Lord would answer my request: Someone would drop the money (equivalent to twenty-five cents in the U.S.). I would find it and be able to pay my bus fare to the bank. To show how little faith I had—even though I expected God to work—I got up in plenty of time to walk to the bank in case the money didn't come.

When I left the house it was dark. All the way to the bus stop I searched for the twenty-five cents I knew would be there. I got to the corner and looked around. I watched people fumble for their change. I searched the ground. I looked everywhere, but found no money.

Maybe the Lord's quarter was not at this bus stop, I thought. Since another bus stop was located several blocks away, I walked to that one. I searched and searched, but no money was to be found. There was one more bus I could take into town. That stop was about eight blocks down the road. The money just had to be at that one.

I had walked about three blocks in the fog and dark when I heard someone trying to push a car out of a garage. He was huffing and puffing but couldn't push it out. I offered to help, and between the two of us we pushed the car out of the garage. As the car rolled down a little hill, the man started it up and he disappeared into the fog.

I continued on my way to the final bus stop still without any money. Then, suddenly in the fog, I heard a car idling. It was the fellow I had helped. He opened the window, apologized for not offering me a ride, and asked where I was going. When I told him, he said he worked at the bank across the street and would be glad to give me a ride.

This story may not be earth-shattering, but the answer to my prayer excited me. It was only worth a quarter, but to me it was a tremendous test. For the first time, I had experienced God getting through my doubts and answering prayer.

Little Faith to Big Faith

Many years later when my evangelistic team and I were conducting a crusade in Lima, Peru, we wanted to televise it. The team member directing the crusade wrote, "Luis, we've got to have money to nail down the contract."

I wrote back, "Sign the contract. We don't have any money, but I believe the Lord's going to send it." They signed the contract.

Our missions account was actually $500 in the red. As we prayed, I had faith that God was going to send the money. The crusade began—the first night, second night, third night—and we still didn't have the $2,500 we needed. The station manager had no idea we didn't have a cent to pay for the program.

On the fourth day a cable came from my wife, Pat. "Praise the Lord," she wrote. "Longhill Chapel in Chatham, New Jersey, has sent in $2,500 for television." The church didn't even know we needed the money.

It took practice and experience in faith to move from that first answer to prayer worth only twenty-five cents to the $2,500 answer to prayer. I had to step out and walk on water many times in the years that separated those two events. Most importantly, I would never have discovered the excitement and blessing of walking by faith if I had never stepped out in the first place.

The exciting thing about beginning to practice walking by faith is that God delights in giving us these experiences. Maybe we sometimes ask silly things. What right did Peter have to expect to walk on water? Yet the Lord told him to come ahead and experience the reward for his faith.

Step out and begin to walk on water. No matter what area of your life you've been wondering about, believe that the Lord will answer your little faith. Your little faith will bring you excitement and, of course, little faith becomes big faith when we begin to practice it day after day.

Chapter 3

WHAT NOW, LORD?

My wife, Pat, in an article for a British magazine, wrote that the best thing to give someone who has lost a child or who has gone through surgery or who is experiencing a crisis is a well-selected, Spirit-led Scripture passage.

What a response her article received from the readers of that Christian magazine. Many people wrote letters to the editor, and some of them really surprised us.

One letter, in particular, stays with me. It was from a woman who said that when her twenty-one-year-old son was run over by a car the last thing she wanted was a Bible verse thrown at her. Instead, she wanted someone to hug her and hold her. Though a hug provides some measure of comfort, if we fully realized the living power of God's Word, we would value a Bible verse as much or more than a hug.

Everyone has to come to terms with the Bible—not just as a book, but as a living message, a living word from God. We cannot really know Jesus Christ unless we accept the Word of God in its fullness. Then we can begin to enjoy the Christian life. This is the next step Peter must take.

Learning to accept the authority of the Word of God and to obey it can be a perplexing process. Scripture divides and tests all those who come in contact with it.

Christ often used very controversial teachings to shake people up. Sometimes it seems He deliberately intended to shock people. The following passage, which records the turning point in Peter's life, illustrates what I mean.

THE FOURTH STEP

God Claims Complete Authority

In John 6:48–69 Jesus Christ says,

"I myself am the bread of life. Your forefathers ate manna in the desert, and they died. This is bread that comes down from Heaven, so that a man may eat it and not die. I myself am the living bread which came down from Heaven, and if anyone eats this bread he will live forever. The bread which I will give is my body and I shall give it for the life of the world."

This led to a fierce argument among the Jews, some of them saying, "How can this man give us his body to eat?"

So Jesus said to them: "Unless you do eat the body of the Son of Man and drink his blood, you are not really living at all. The man who eats my flesh and drinks my blood has eternal life and I will raise him up when the last day comes. For my body is real food and my blood is real drink. The man who eats my body and drinks my blood shares my life and I share his. Just as the living Father sent me and I am alive because of the Father, so the man who lives on me will live because of me. This is the bread which came down from Heaven! It is not like the manna which your forefathers used to eat, and died. The man who eats this bread will live forever."

Jesus said all these things while teaching in the synagogue at Capernaum. Many of his disciples heard him say these things, and commented. "This is hard teaching indeed; who could accept that?"

Then Jesus, knowing intuitively that his disciples were complaining about what he had just said, went on: "Is this too much for you? Then what would happen if you were to see the Son of Man going up to the place where he was before? It is the Spirit which gives life. The flesh will not help you. The things which I have told you are spiritual and are life. But some of you will not believe me."

For Jesus knew from the beginning which of his followers did not trust him and who was the man who would betray him. Then he added, "This is why I said to you, 'No one can come to me unless my Father puts it into his heart to come.'"

As a consequence of this, many of his disciples withdrew and no longer followed him. So Jesus said to the twelve, "And are you too wanting to go away?"

"Lord," answered Simon Peter, "who else should we go to? Your words have the ring of eternal life! And we believe and are convinced that you are the holy one of God."

Jesus replied, "Did I not choose you twelve—and one of
you has the devil in his heart?"

He was speaking of Judas, the son of Simon Iscariot,
one of the twelve, who was planning to betray him.

Sifting and Testing

In the above passage Jesus was talking to the Jews.
Many people were following Him—people who had
seen His miracles, people who had been fed by the
bread He had multiplied. Following a miracle worker
is exciting, and Jesus had attracted quite an audience.

But after Jesus had performed those miracles and
showed people some of the excitement of walking
with Him, He began to sift through and test His
admirers. He used some very hard language and difficult concepts in speaking to them.

For instance, He says, "If you want to have eternal
life, you've got to eat my flesh and drink my blood."
This statement shocked His followers.

The first ones to drop out were unbelievers. They
didn't want to have a thing to do with Jesus, and His
controversial teachings gave them good reason to
conclude that this man was out of His mind.

The unbelieving Jews weren't the only ones who
dropped out. Jesus Christ's statement troubled many
of those who had begun to call themselves His disciples. In verse 60 we're told, "Many of his disciples
heard him say these things, and commented, 'This is
hard teaching indeed; who could accept that?'" The
Lord knew exactly what He was doing. He was testing
to find out if His followers really believed He had the
answers.

Every one of us, even those of us brought up in a Christian atmosphere, has to confront this question. Does Jesus Christ have the answer? Many face this issue when they go to secular colleges and meet unbelieving professors who have the audacity to doubt Jesus Christ, question the Bible, and make fun of Christianity. Students brought up in Christian homes suddenly have to make a decision: Who has the answers? Is it Jesus Christ or is it this educated, self-sufficient professor?

We all have to face this traumatic, but essential, experience. Until we determine who our authority is, we are a long way from maturity. Until we accept the authority of Jesus Christ over our rational processes, we are still floundering babies.

I was in London, England, for a fourteen-week crusade, and every night before I started preaching, I would lift up my Bible before the crowds and say, "This is the Word of the Lord. Absolutely perfect, 100 percent trustworthy. No mistakes, no errors. Listen to the Word of the Lord." Afterward, I received letters from several ministers who were angry at my words. Why? They didn't believe the Bible was the perfect Word of God.

We have to come to the place where we forget what the professor says, what the psychologist says, what the historian says, and even what the pastor says when it conflicts with Christ's words. As Christians we must accept the Bible in its entirety as the inspired Word of God, believe all it says, and love it.

This doesn't imply an irrational acceptance without thought and intelligent question. It does mean that we accept the authority of Jesus Christ and His Word in the face of unbelieving attacks on His principles.

After losing many followers, we might expect Jesus to drop the issue, but He wasn't finished. Some of the disciples had dropped out, so He called the intimate group—the Twelve—and asked them if they wanted to leave also.

You see, the issue was not the precise wording of the doctrine of eating His body and drinking His blood. The issue was following Jesus Christ all the way even when what He says offends our sensibilities. Jesus was asking, "Are you willing to follow Me even if what I say sounds irrational?

When Jesus asked that question, Peter said, "Lord, who else should we go to? Your words have the ring of eternal life!" (John 6:68). With those words, Peter settled for himself the question of who has the answers.

Accepting the Right Authority

I'm amazed how many Christians turn to the world for advice. It's as if they believe the world's way of doing things is better than God's way. They listen to what the world says is right and wrong, instead of listening to Scripture. The Bible gives them this advice: "Do not love the world or anything in the world. If anyone loves the world, the love of the Father is not in him" (1 John 2:15, NIV).

We should listen to worldly people as little as possible, especially in the areas of philosophy, psychology, religion, and in all those areas where they know little or nothing. In some of the sciences they're as bright or brighter than we are, but when it comes to anything philosophical, sociological, psychiatric, and spiritual —don't waste your time with the unbelievers.

So many of the people in the mass media that we pay attention to live defeated personal lives because they neglect the most important dimension of reality—the spiritual truths of Scripture.

I was seated next to a middle-aged business executive on a plane flight, and we began to talk. When he asked my occupation, I told him I was a traveling evangelist.

He told me, "I suppose you're against adultery. I'll tell you something about marriage. In the old days men and women died a lot earlier, so it was easy to say 'til death us do part.' Nowadays if you stay with the same woman, it's for fifty-five years and you get bored. You have to play the field."

What do we say in situations like that? Many people today are using arguments for unfaithfulness or for this or for that that seem persuasive. If we begin to listen to what they say, we can't avoid making mistakes. Disoriented by the ways of the world, we can start considering just about anything.

But just because an argument is persuasive doesn't mean you and I should buy into it. Just because someone has a degree or speaks with authority or has his or her own talk show shouldn't influence us to uncritically accept what he or she says. God gives us specific commands to follow, one being not to commit adultery. Even if God doesn't explain His reasons, we obey because He says so.

Christians have to decide who they are going to follow. If you still doubt the word of Jesus Christ and His authority, don't be surprised if you flounder and vacillate when you read the pseudointellectuals who deny the existence of God, who deny the reality of Jesus Christ, and then dare to tell you how to live and make decisions. Anyone who denies these basic truths should never be our authority.

Peter settled the issue for himself when he decided to stay with Christ and His teachings. Paul, in 2 Timothy 3:16 states, "All Scripture is God-breathed and is useful for teaching, rebuking, correcting and training in righteousness" (NIV).

Once you have settled the question of Christ's authority over you and have given Him supremacy in your life, then you can read and listen to others intelligently and critically and not be shaken. You can judge everything the "authorities" say in the light of Scripture.

When you settle the authority of Jesus Christ, you are free to be a real intellectual, not a pseudointellectual who denies the existence of God and the authority of the Word. Because you know God personally, because you have settled the issue of authority in your life, you can comfortably accept statements that are consistent with eternal truths and reject those that are not. Your faith cannot be shattered or shaken because Jesus Christ is the last word for you.

Can you, like Peter, accept the hard things of the Lord as well as the sweet rewards and blessings? Your attitude toward the words of Jesus is a good measuring rod of maturity.

Scripture records many hard things that are serious stumbling blocks to some believers. They just can't accept God asking the people of Israel to wipe out a whole tribe, or other difficult commands. God has very good reasons behind His words. Those who have the audacity to question the wisdom of God are suggesting they are more morally enlightened than God Himself.

We often think we are very mature and spiritual when we question the hard things of the Lord, but the opposite is true. We simply show our spiritual baby-hood. Our questions demonstrate our lack of development and knowledge of Scripture. Challenging God's authority is a manifestation of our immaturity.

God never makes mistakes. When we challenge His hard sayings, we are really challenging His authority. We have not settled the issue of authority if we still retain the right to pick and choose what we like from the Scriptures.

The sooner we accept His Word by faith, the sooner we'll be delivered from the kind of chastisement and discipline Peter had to go through. Even after his commitment to stay with Christ, Peter challenged the Lord's authority in his heart. He still has much to learn.

THE FIFTH STEP
God Reveals Christ as His Son

Billy Graham tells the story of a visit he and his wife, Ruth, took to China before Christianity really exploded there. They were speaking in a small church and afterward a man came up to talk with Billy. Through a translator this fellow asked, "What did you say the name was of that man who died on a cross?"

Billy answered, "His name was Jesus." The man said, "So that was His name. I've believed in Him all my life, but I didn't know His name."

That touched me. The revelation that Jesus Christ is God is the answer the world is waiting to hear.

In Matthew 16:13–20 the disciples, for the first time, declare their belief in this truth:

> When Jesus reached the Caesarea-Philippi district he asked his disciples a question. "Who do people say the Son of Man is?"
>
> "Well, some say John the Baptist," they told him. "Some say Elijah, others Jeremiah or one of the prophets."
>
> "But what about you?" he said to them. "Who do you say that I am?"
>
> Simon Peter answered, "You? You are Christ, the Son of the living God!"
>
> "Simon, son of Jonah, you are a fortunate man indeed!" said Jesus, "for it was not your own nature but my Heavenly Father who has revealed this truth to you! Now I tell you that you are Peter the rock, and it is on this rock that I am going to found my Church, and the powers of death will never prevail against it. I will give you the keys of the kingdom of Heaven; whatever you forbid on earth will be what is forbidden in Heaven and whatever you permit on earth will be what is permitted in Heaven!" Then he impressed on his disciples that they should not tell anyone that he was Christ.

Scripture here gives us the *revelation of Christ as God*. How excited Jesus must have been when these men had finally begun to understand who He was. And when Christ asked His men who they thought He was, Peter gave Him the answer He was looking for. "You are Christ, the Son of the living God!"

Measure of Maturity

Our hearts accept the revelation of Jesus Christ as God only through the work of the Holy Spirit. A young woman of twenty-five decided to attend a family conference at which I was speaking. Though a member of a church, this woman lived as if she never heard the gospel. Bitterly angry at her father, unhappy with her mother, she began playing around with men and women.

Tired of her angry and immoral lifestyle, this woman listened intently to the music and Bible study at the conference, and God got her attention. Unsure whether she ever had invited Jesus Christ into her heart, the woman repented of her sin and committed her life to God. Today, she is serving God as a missionary in Mozambique, Africa. Understanding that Jesus Christ is the Son of the living God radically changed her life.

Being raised in a Christian home does not automatically make a person's heart receptive, neither can we argue this revelation into a person. We can only quote verses and make a theological appeal. The Holy Spirit must reveal to a person the truth of Jesus Christ as God, or a man or a woman will not and cannot believe.

The Lord Jesus said in Matthew 11:25, "I praise you, Father, Lord of heaven and earth, because you have hidden these things from the wise and learned, and revealed them to little children" (NIV). Humility must reign in our hearts before Christ can reveal Himself as the Son of God to us.

Accepting Christ isn't a question of saying, "Well, I kind of like Him. My mother believed in Him. When I was young I used to get on my knees beside my bed and pray to Jesus. It felt good, but I don't know if He's the Son of God."

If that is where you stand, you are in bad shape. Either Jesus Christ is who He said He is, or He is the biggest deceiver who ever lived. He claimed to be God the Son revealed in the flesh. Salvation cannot occur until a sinner comes to that place where he or she wholly accepts that Jesus Christ is the anointed one, the Christ, the Son of the living God. The greatest moment in the life of Peter came when he said, "You are the Christ, the Son of the living God."

With this realization, Peter stepped into a greater measure of maturity. As a result of that step, the Lord Jesus confirmed His promise to Peter. He said, in effect, "Now you indeed *are* Peter. Now you *are* the rock. Your confession confirms that you are standing on solid ground."

Spiritual maturity begins for the believer when the full impact of who Christ is becomes real. Spiritual childhood ends when men and women understand that this living Christ who dwells within them is more than a Savior. He is the Son of the living God.

This realization—that the living Christ lives within Luis Palau—changed my spiritual life. I tell you, that was the beginning of a new, real life for me.

The Bible teaches that a person who is joined to the Lord becomes one spirit with Him. Suddenly I'm not going through life on my own with a little wisdom from the outside. I'm indwelt and controlled by the Son of God. Such a miracle cannot help but change a person's life.

Commission of Authority

Christ not only blessed Peter but *gave him a promise.* Christ clearly explains the commission He gave to Peter in Matthew 16:18:

> You are Peter the rock, and it is on this rock that I am going to found my Church, and the powers of death will never prevail against it. I will give you the keys of the kingdom of Heaven; whatever you forbid on earth will be what is forbidden in Heaven and whatever you permit on earth will be what is permitted in Heaven!

Matthew 18:17–20 says,

> And if he still won't pay any attention, tell the matter to the church. And if he won't even listen to the church then he must be to you just like a pagan—or a tax collector!
>
> Believe me, whatever you forbid upon earth will be what is forbidden in Heaven, and whatever you permit on earth will be what is permitted in Heaven.
>
> And I tell you once more that if two of you on earth agree in asking for anything it will be granted to you by my

Heavenly Father. For wherever two or three people come together in my name, I am there, right among them!

Notice the tremendous authority Christ gave to Peter. On the faith that Peter represented, Christ would build His church. The real church, the body of Christ, is built on people who believe Jesus Christ is God the Son. The deity of Christ is the rock, and all who believe can lay claim to the authority Christ gave Peter after his confession. We can claim that authority because Jesus is God and dwells within us.

During our crusade in India, tens of thousands came to hear the gospel and thousands trusted Christ. The response clearly showed God's absolute power over all creation, even in this area where demonic activity is so obvious.

On one occasion while speaking to several thousand young people, I felt that either Satan was at work, or some of the professing Christians there were secretly living in serious sin. I stopped in the middle of my message to address this issue. The result was incredible. The atmosphere, which had been unbearable, became almost awesomely silent.

The Bible says we can overcome the enemy of God, Satan and his demons, because "the one is greater who is in you than the one who is in the world" (1 John 4:4, NIV).

We can stand against Satan and his schemes, and even thwart his plans, but we must be fully prepared and rely completely on God's power. This isn't a game. Satan isn't *pretending* to want to destroy us. But

Satan's demise is certain. In the end our all-powerful God will defeat him. And this same God is living inside of the hearts of all believers. That's why we can stand firm when Satan attempts to destroy us. Christ is the victor in me!

What did Jesus mean by the keys of the kingdom of heaven? The keys are an expression, an example that our authority in Christ is not limited to earth. Whatever we permit on earth is permitted in heaven, whatever we bind here is bound there. That is authority! I see three implications in the keys—*privilege, authority,* and *responsibility.*

Think of the *privilege* of having the keys to the kingdom of God. When we take a Bible and witness to someone in the name of Jesus Christ, we exercise the privileges of the keys of the kingdom.

I think of John Wesley who lived 250 years ago. As a young man, Wesley discovered "instantaneous conversion and immediate assurance," and it made an impact on all of Britain. The Lord soon impressed upon Wesley the mission of preaching the gospel. During the next 50 years Wesley traveled some 250,000 miles throughout the United Kingdom and preached 40,000 sermons. His message was always the same, urging men and women to make sure of their salvation. He understood the great privilege God has given to us to preach the gospel.

Second, we can speak with *authority.* We don't have to be apologetic or unsure. We can say with boldness that Jesus Christ is God's Son and that He changes lives and gives peace with God.

A newsman who had met Billy Graham many times wrote these words: "The thing that shakes me up about Billy Graham is his arrogant humility." What an interesting description. That is what our authority in Christ permits each one of us to have—arrogant humility.

In addition to privilege and authority, the keys teach of our *responsibility*. Some of us would rather pass responsibility on to ministers and teachers. We would rather be little anonymous nobodies. When we realize the reality of the indwelling Christ, we grow in Him. The Bible has authority over us. We have the right, God's authority, to speak in the name of the Lord Jesus Christ. But more, we have the responsibility.

For me, this exciting responsibility comes to the fore while doing crusade evangelism. It is such a blessing to move into a city and, in the name of Jesus Christ, claim that community for God. Because we come in the name of Jesus Christ and have the keys to the kingdom, we have the authority, the privilege, and the responsibility to move in as His representatives.

One of the special guests who sang at our crusade in southern California was Darlene Koldenhoven. You may not know Darlene Koldenhoven. I'm certainly no expert on Hollywood, and until my staff told me, I didn't know that Darlene starred in *Sister Act* with Whoopi Goldberg. During the crusade, on Friday night, Darlene sang "Ready for a Miracle," leading the crowd in foot stompin' praise.

But Darlene didn't come alone that night. She brought several friends to hear the gospel. Darlene says one woman came searching for and finding God. And another friend and her daughter came with Darlene Friday night, returned on Saturday, and said they wanted to know more about church and the Lord. Darlene says she had been praying for a vehicle to bring these women in, and the crusade was it. She understood she had a responsibility to reach people for Jesus Christ where God had placed her.

The same is true for all men and women, whether they are business people, homemakers, industrial workers, or students. God has placed them wherever they are, not just as laborers or parents or students, but as His children, bearers of the keys of the kingdom.

When Peter was given this commission of incredible authority, he had reached a beautiful and exhilarating high point in his life. But, from here on the whole tone of his maturing process was going to change. Peter wasn't ready to handle the responsibilities. Peter, like many of us, once again had to come to the end of himself before Christ could take him deeper.

Chapter 4

OBSTACLES TO MATURITY

In our journey to becoming effective and fruitful Christians, we all encounter obstacles. The spiritual life is often an agonizing progression of thrilling blessings and heartbreaking failures.

I remember arriving in Costa Rica with my wife, excited to finally begin our life as missionaries. Because Pat had to attend language school to learn Spanish, we began looking for a housekeeper. None could be found. So Pat went to school while I stayed home and took care of the twins for three long weeks.

After a couple of days, I couldn't take it any longer. Impatiently, I told the Lord, "Is this what I came here for? Here I am on the mission field, but instead of preaching and winning souls, I'm stuck at home, day after day—burping babies and changing messy diapers!"

Self-reliance had once again reared its ugly head. I thought I knew better than God what He wanted me to be doing for those three weeks, and I made sure I told Him my plans. The Lord had to remind me to trust His perfect will and perfect timing.

We all will encounter obstacles to maturity. We can't speed up the process. We can't learn obedience and trust without Christ's dealing with us. We are so stubborn, so rebellious, so self-confident that the Lord has to teach us to face ourselves, not as others see us, but as He sees us. Only then will we realize in abject humility how much we need Him.

Jesus Christ must deal with the obstacles to maturity in your life and my life and remove them one by one. When God allows us to go through troubles and problems, He is trying to remove from our lives those things that stand in the way of the growing up process.

THE FIRST OBSTACLE
Refusal to Take Up the Cross

Peter has come a long way. We have watched him progress from his first encounter with Christ to the great moment when he learned about faith and walked on water. Then he learned about trusting the Word of God and accepting the hard sayings of Jesus. Finally we watched as he realized and testified that

Jesus Christ is the Son of the living God and was rewarded with the keys of the kingdom.

Unfortunately, Peter had not yet encountered the obstacles that would test his faith and obedience. When he did meet up with them, he failed so dramatically that his behavior might suggest he wasn't really a Christian in the first place.

We read about the first obstacle Peter encountered in Matthew 16:21–27.

> From that time onward Jesus began to explain to his disciples that he would have to go to Jerusalem, and endure much suffering from the elders, chief priests and scribes, and finally be killed; and be raised to life again on the third day.
>
> Then Peter took him on one side and started to remonstrate with him over this. "God bless you, Master! Nothing like this must happen to you!" Then Jesus turned round and said to Peter, "Out of my way, Satan! . . . You stand right in my path, Peter, when you look at things from man's point of view and not from God's."
>
> Then Jesus said to his disciples: "If anyone wants to follow in my footsteps he must give up all right to himself, take up his cross and follow me. For the man who wants to save his life will lose it; but the man who loses his life for my sake will find it. For what good is it for a man to gain the whole world at the price of his own soul? What could a man offer to buy back his soul once he had lost it?
>
> "For the Son of Man will come in the glory of his Father and in the company of his angels and then he will repay every man for what he has done."

The Unredeemed Mind

Not long before, the Lord Jesus made tremendous promises to Peter because of his confession of faith. Now Peter suddenly had the audacity to turn around and dictate to the Lord. The Lord was telling His disciples about the cross. He was telling them how He would have to shed His blood for the redemption of the world.

Peter, expressing great ignorance and arrogance, dared to contradict his Lord's teaching. Perhaps he felt his new authority gave him the right to question Christ.

Peter was not the first, nor will he be the last to tell Christ what is good and what isn't good. Many people do just that because they cannot accept certain things from the Bible. According to a recent Barna Research Group poll, only 55 percent of Americans today believe the Bible's teachings are "totally accurate." Many people throw out certain passages and question many others.

Some people want to discard the teachings about hell. Others find the doctrine of the blood of the cross particularly offensive. The cross, they say, is a carry-over from an unsophisticated culture, and to talk of dying on a cross and shedding blood repulses a cultured and educated person.

But the cross isn't repulsive to a cultured, educated person who recognizes the depth of his own depravity, his own self-centeredness, and his sin. Only when men and women see themselves as God sees them will they realize it's only in the blood of Christ that they can find the hope they seek.

Christ used this occasion to show that the gospel is diametrically opposed to unredeemed human nature. Romans 8:6–8 tells us, "The mind of sinful man is death, but the mind controlled by the Spirit is life and peace; the sinful mind is hostile to God. It does not submit to God's law, nor can it do so. Those controlled by the sinful nature cannot please God" (NIV).

The unredeemed mind is hostile to the gospel. We can't stand the message of redemption through Christ's blood until the Holy Spirit comes and takes over. The human mind rebels against the thought that the Son of God gave His blood on the cross. "Mankind can't be that bad," some people reason. "Surely there must be another way to God," and so on. We rebel against it just as Peter did.

Christ will not leave a Christian in error long, however. He uses our mistakes to continue our education. Christ met Peter head on at every turn, as He does us.

I used to have a next-door neighbor with whom I would chat from time to time. But I didn't share the gospel with him. "After all," I thought, "he seems completely immune to the problems of life."

Eventually, though, my neighbor changed. The joy seemed to have left his face. His marriage was souring. I felt the need to talk with him, but I didn't want to meddle in his life. I went about my business and left for an evangelistic crusade. After all, that was the polite thing to do.

When I returned home, I learned my neighbor had killed himself. I was heartbroken. I knew I should have talked to him about following Christ. But because of false courtesy—because I followed a social norm—I didn't do it. You can believe I tried not to make that mistake again.

When Peter objected to Christ's talking about the cross and His sacrifice, he might have expected a grateful response from Christ. After all, Peter was demonstrating his love and protection of his Lord. But the Lord Jesus did not commend him. Instead, He chastised Peter for thinking only as a human being, and letting Satan influence him.

Peter must have been stunned to be rebuked so dramatically. The rebuke came because Peter had not yet learned that he must die to self, to his own wishes, preferences, and opinions, and must let Christ rule totally without contradiction and without opposition.

Opposing Christ and His redemptive work is Satan's sworn duty. No wonder Christ's response to Peter's concern was an uncompromising rebuke of Satan's influence on him.

Bearing the Cross

Jesus not only spoke of His death, but He also taught that death is the doorway to life. He said, "If anyone wants to follow in my footsteps he must give up all right to himself, take up his cross and follow me" (Matt. 16:24).

What is the cross? As I understand it, bearing my cross means that every time God's will clashes with my will, I choose His. Cross bearing does not mean tolerating an aggressive relative or enduring a financial problem, troublesome as those things might be. It goes much deeper than that. When your self-will and your confident attitude oppose God's will, and you humbly choose to follow Him, you have taken up the cross.

When I was in Latvia for an evangelistic crusade, I met an outstanding hero of the faith named Josef Bondarenko. As a young man, Josef had begun preaching the gospel, gaining the title, "the Billy Graham of Russia."

At age 22, he was arrested by the KGB for his preaching and put in jail for more than three years. He was then freed, but a year later the KGB jailed him again. After gaining his freedom, the same thing happened again. Three times, for a total of ten and one-half years, Josef was imprisoned. By human standards, the best years of his life were wasted. But his faithful preaching of the gospel resulted in many lives changed for eternity.

During his third prison sentence, a KGB colonel called Josef into his private office. The colonel said, "Josef, I'm the man who put you in jail these three times. There was no reason except you insisted on preaching the gospel. Yet, through these many years, you have never cursed us. In fact, people have heard you pray for us. Do you think there's any hope for me? Will God ever forgive me?"

Josef had every right, in human terms, to be angry and bitter. He could have refused to share how Jesus Christ can change a life. Instead, Josef took up the cross. He humbly chose to follow God's will and not his own. The result? Josef led the colonel to the Lord.

Taking up the cross is the hardest lesson for a Christian to learn. Thousands of Christians are still spiritual babies because they have stopped at this obstacle and will not go any further. They cannot accept the cross of Jesus Christ.

When you surrender to God your will and all that makes you proud and arrogant, you have overcome a great obstacle to growth. But you must be willing to say, "Lord, everything I have—intellect, social standing, the ability to make money—all this is a gift from You. You graciously gave me these abilities and I thank You for them. But, Lord, I want Your will and Your way in my life."

When you give up self, life begins to flow. Remember Galatians 2:20? "I have been crucified with Christ and I no longer live, but Christ lives in me. The life I live in the body, I live by faith in the Son of God, who loved me and gave himself for me" (NIV).

Overflowing Life

When a person finally comes to the cross and chooses God's will against his own, he comes alive. As the indwelling Christ begins to take over, his life begins to overflow. Jesus promised this in John 7:37–38 when He said, "If anyone is thirsty, let him come to me and drink. Whoever believes in me, as the Scripture has said, streams of living water will flow from within him" (NIV).

In other words, when you come to the end of yourself and say, "I am thirsty, I am needy, I don't have all that it takes," it is then the Holy Spirit takes over and the water of life begins to flow.

When Christians are Spirit filled, they are at peace with the Lord and at peace with themselves. They are not stiff, uptight, and self-centered. They have a way about them that says, "Jesus Christ is in control of my life."

We all can know if the Holy Spirit is flowing through us or if we are trying to do it on our own. A quietness, a peace, and a reality saturates the life of a man or woman within whom Christ is in control. This peacefulness is the natural, normal state for the believer.

Until we remove the obstacles that prevent us from realizing full obedience to Christ, we will be unfulfilled, restless, and discontented Christians. We have no alternative to learning to take up the cross.

THE SECOND OBSTACLE

Uncontrolled Tongue

Bill Peterson, former football coach for Florida State, was well known for the mistakes he made in speech. After he died at age seventy-three, several of his famous, or should I say infamous, lines were recorded in the newspaper.

"The greatest thing just happened," he said. "I got indicted into the Florida Sports Hall of Fame and they gave me a standing observation." Here's another one: "I'm the football coach and don't you remember it!" Another time he said, "We can beat this team. All we have to do is capitalize on our mistakes."

You know, our mouths always seem to get us in trouble. Sometimes we make small slips of the tongue, like Bill Peterson made. Other times we fail big time.

One of the signs that shows Christ is not in control of our lives is a loose tongue, saying things that hurt people. Peter was guilty of this.

Matthew 17:2–8 tells us,

There [Jesus'] whole appearance changed before their eyes, his face shining like the sun and his clothes as white as light. Then Moses and Elijah were seen talking to Jesus.

"Lord," exclaimed Peter, "it is wonderful for us to be here! If you like I could put up three shelters, one each for you and Moses and Elijah—"

But while he was still talking a bright cloud overshadowed them and a voice came out of the cloud: "This is my dearly loved Son in whom I am well pleased. Listen to him!"

When they heard this voice the disciples fell on their faces, overcome with fear. Then Jesus came up to them and touched them. "Get up and don't be frightened," he said. And as they raised their eyes there was no one to be seen but Jesus himself.

Peter, James, and John witnessed a wonderful scene—the Son of God transfigured like He is going to be in glory, accompanied by Moses and Elijah. Jesus and His companions were talking about the cross, about the redemption that was going to take place in Jerusalem, about the most solemn and momentous event of history—the Son of God dying for the sins of humankind. What a glorious revelation of the presence of God.

But Peter, with an uncontrolled tongue, dared again to interrupt his Lord. "Lord, it is wonderful for us to be here! If you like I could put up three shelters, one each for you and Moses and Elijah!"

The "I" was coming to the fore. Peter offered to handle all the details and erect three monuments. But, before he was through with his little speech, God interrupted. A bright cloud came and covered them and the voice of the Father said, "This is my dearly loved Son in whom I am well pleased. Listen to him!" God the Father was saying, "Peter, be still. This is the Son of God. Keep quiet and listen to Him." His own sincerity must have made God's rebuke doubly shocking to Peter.

We are all guilty of this. In our arrogance and self-confidence, we take so little time to listen to God. We think so much of our opinions and sincerely think God will be pleased with them. Many of us suffer with the same affliction: sincere ignorance. We mean right. We want to please the Lord, and yet everything we do seems to bring rebuke instead of blessing. Uncrucified pride gets us in trouble, and sometimes Christ is forced to use strong tactics to break through it.

Shock Treatment

Perhaps the Lord's words to Peter seem a little harsh: first He called Peter Satan, and then He later tells him to be still. But sometimes we need a dose of shock treatment, which is a good method if done in love.

Two men in my life have been used by God to deal me tremendous blows, and their blows straightened out my life.

One of them is Ray Stedman. Through him God brought me from Argentina to the United States. I knew Ray loved me like a son, and I admired and respected him like a father. This man had more of the character and temperament of Jesus Christ than any man I've ever met, even under all kinds of stress and pressure.

His life was quite an example for me. Like Peter, I sincerely wanted to serve Christ, but I knew next to nothing about the indwelling Christ when I first arrived in the States. I did not understand that it was not Luis Palau, but Christ in me, who had to do the job.

Like many young men who want to serve Christ, I thought quite a bit of myself. I was bilingual, having been educated in British schools and in the Cambridge program. I had led Sunday school and preached on street corners. I felt a great sense of pride when I gave little messages. I felt I knew a great deal about what I was saying.

One day Ray told me he wanted to talk to me about something. He knew I had begun dating Pat, who later became my wife, and had failed to inform a woman I had been dating in Argentina. Many times he had encouraged me to write this woman, but I never did.

He brought up the subject again that day. I said, "Don't worry. When I get back home, I'll talk to a few people and get out of it."

Ray put his arm around me and said, "You know, my son, you really think you can solve any problem with that mouth." I started to object, but he shut me off. "Luis, one of these days you are going to dig a hole so deep with your mouth that not even God will be able to pull you out of it—unless you shape up."

That was a blow! But Ray went on very lovingly and said, "Luis, you are so proud and cocky that it oozes out of your pores and you don't even realize it!"

When he said that, I knew it was God's voice. I needed no confirmation. My friend was right. That brought a turning point in my life.

Proverbs 27:6 says, "Wounds of a friend can be trusted; but an enemy multiplies kisses" (NIV). When someone really loves you and sees weaknesses in you, he or she is going to put an arm around you and let you have it. Fortunate is the individual who has such friends.

When I got married a few months later, Pat and I were sent to Detroit, Michigan, to study psychology. The Lord had another lesson waiting for me there. I call this the final "bringing me to the cross once and for all" blow.

We were missionary interns working at a local church. I was supposed to help the pastor. In return, the church gave us lodging in the attic of an elderly woman's home. She was aging and a bit eccentric. She refused to put a lock on the door of our room and would walk in on us unannounced whenever she pleased. We had been married just three weeks and young married couples like their privacy.

I became so angry about the situation that, instead of going to Fred Renich, the director of the missionary internship program, I wrote to the director of Overseas Crusades who oversaw this program. I threatened to leave the internship program. In no uncertain terms I said if he wanted to throw me out of Overseas Crusades he could go right ahead, but to get me and my wife out of that attic!

Overseas Crusades, of course, wrote immediately to Fred and said, "What are you doing to this young couple? We sent them to you to train and you put them in an impossible situation!"

Fred acted quickly. However, he saw beyond my actions to my arrogance, lack of humility, and immature Christian character that my actions exhibited. He called me into his office and said, "Luis, I have a letter here telling me to get you out of that attic. You will be out of the apartment by tomorrow. But I'd like to ask why you didn't come to me instead of writing to your director?"

"I wanted to be sure I'd get action," I said.

"The line of authority would be through me," Fred said. "This way you made me look like a clown in front of your director. It hurt me." He went on. "Let me tell you something. If you look at your wife, Pat, you will notice she is quiet, easy-going, and pliable. If you don't let Christ take over in your life, you are going to step all over her throughout your life. You will crush her and never even know it. Think back on your life. I'm willing to bet you, Luis, that all along the pathway of your life are skeletons of people you have stepped on and hurt because of your aggressive temperament. And you don't even know it."

I returned to my attic apartment somewhat stunned. Everything Fred had said was accurate. I thought over my life and remembered a number of people whom I had cruelly injured with my pride and self-righteousness. I remembered how many Sunday school teachers just dropped out of the Sunday school program because of the demands I imposed as superintendent. I thought I was being rigorous and disciplined in my expectations. I realized now that I unknowingly was stepping on them in my egotism and pride.

The shock treatment Jesus Christ gave to Peter was necessary. Jesus used it to show Peter his real self and make him realize that in and of himself, he was an arrogant and useless character.

Peter refused to understand that he couldn't have his own way and God's will at the same time. He couldn't let go of self and let Christ be all. All the lessons Peter learned—the lessons God used Ray Stedman and Fred Renich to teach me—were God's way of telling him and me that Christ must have preeminence in our lives.

Let Him control you and you will be the kind of person you want to be—the kind of person God wants you to be. Praise God for shock treatments!

Chapter 5

MORE OBSTACLES

During a telecast of *Night Talk*, our call-in evangelistic program, I talked with a pastor's wife whose daughter had been murdered. In a separate incident, her son was beaten and left for dead. For nine years she had been living with those memories, and the hate she felt toward the attackers was so strong she felt she couldn't overcome it.

Who could blame this woman for hating? But, as she discovered, hate was eating her alive and creating an obstacle to her spiritual growth. She was not experiencing the joy and peace Jesus wants all believers to experience.

Jesus Christ said in John 10:10, "I have come that they may have life, and have it to the full" (NIV). Christ wants every man and woman to live an abundant life, a joyful life, a truthful life, a happy life.

When Jesus Christ takes hold of believers, His objective is, as soon as possible, to get them to grow up, to make them real men and women of God. Christ came so that we could be conformed to His image. He wants to make us over with His character.

Take a look at the often-quoted promise in Philippians 1:6: "Being confident of this, that he who began a good work in you will carry it on to completion until the day of Christ Jesus" (NIV). Every believer can take great comfort in God's promise to us. When Christ takes over in a life, He will finish the job. What He started, He will finish. If He came all the way to earth, became a man, and allowed Himself to be crucified so we could be forgiven and cleansed, don't you think He plans to finish the job? Of course He does! He is not going to start something and then let go. It cost Him too much.

In Peter we see a man in the process of maturing, in the process of being brought to completion. Every one of us is in that process. How far we have come in that process, however, depends on how willing we have been to let the indwelling Christ take over our lives. As believers, our responsibility is to cooperate with Jesus Christ by willingly letting Him have His way in our lives.

As stubborn as Peter was, he found cooperation difficult to learn. Jesus Christ spent many months bringing him to a place of obedience. The Lord finally had to shock him out of his self-will. But the shocks Peter received caused a healthy breakdown of his old patterns of living. With each new obstacle to maturity

Peter encountered, he learned a greater degree and depth of obedience to his Master. Christ used Peter's failures to teach him—and to teach us—how to walk with God. Peter is an excellent example for studying this process because he failed so dramatically and so often.

THE THIRD OBSTACLE

Unrecognized Defilement

I remember a revival that took place during a week of evangelistic meetings at a church in Cali, Colombia. It was the first time I had seen this kind of confession and brokenness among the people. More than 130 people were saved.

The last Sunday of the campaign, one of the elders of the church stood up in the meeting and began to complain—while 35 of the new believers who had been saved during the week watched and listened.

"Pastor," he said, "I'm upset because my flowers aren't being used to decorate the sanctuary. It was my turn to buy the flowers, but someone else brought flowers and those are the ones being used. I spent my hard-earned money, and it's not even appreciated."

On and on he went, probably unaware that anger and bitterness had defiled his life. He probably felt he was serving God by bringing flowers to church, but I think God was more concerned about correcting his sinful attitude.

Jesus warns us about this attitude in John 13:4–11, when He washed His disciples' feet. He used the situation to teach them, and us, the danger of unrecognized defilement.

In the Middle East, dust was abundant as there were no paved roads. When a person went to a dinner or a party, he or she was expected to bathe before setting out. But on the walk to the host's house, the guest's feet would get dirty. Dusty feet were an unpleasant accompaniment to dinner, especially since those eating did not sit at a table but rather reclined on couches. Customarily a servant of the host washed the guests' feet.

On this occasion, Christ and His disciples had gathered for the final Passover, what we call the Lord's Supper. They had no slaves to wash each other's feet. So, the Lord Jesus Himself took off His outer clothing, rolled up His sleeves, got a basin of water, and kneeled before them to wash their feet.

They all had dust on their feet. They all were defiled. But when Jesus came to Peter, Peter objected to having his feet washed. We are told that Peter said, " 'You must never wash my feet!'

" 'Unless you let me wash you, Peter,' replied Jesus, 'you cannot share my lot.'

" 'Then,' returned Simon Peter, 'please—not just my feet but my hands and my face as well!'" (John 13:8–9).

Peter was sincerely concerned that Christ not kneel to wash his feet. Here was a man with defiled feet, but he wasn't aware of his need. Or if he was aware of his need, he didn't want Christ to remedy it.

We encounter a tremendous obstacle to maturity when we think we are all right—that we don't need to be cleansed daily by the Word of God and by the blood of Jesus Christ. Thousands of Christians believe that they are in great shape, that they have everything under control. They think temptations will trouble only those people who are weak or immature, but they overlook the fact that every believer needs to have his or her feet washed daily.

Defiant Heart

Not only was Peter defiled but he had a defiant heart. Contamination alone did not trouble the Lord. He knows each one of us, and He is not shaken by your contamination or mine. What troubled the Lord was Peter's defiant heart. When Peter objected to having his feet washed, Jesus responded with a strong statement. "Unless you let me wash you, Peter, you cannot share my lot."

What did the Lord mean? He knew of Peter's love and commitment and sincerity.

What the Lord had to teach Peter was that if he was not cleansed from daily defilement—from the impurities of mind, heart, and soul that accrue as he walks through the world—he could have no part in friendship with Christ. Peter could bear no fruit because a contaminated vessel cannot hold or dispense blessing.

Every day we may be defiled by "big" sins or by "small" sins. It doesn't matter. The believer has to return daily to the feet of Jesus Christ and gladly be cleansed and refreshed.

Interestingly, Peter's response to this incident demonstrates his sincerity. When the Lord Jesus said Peter couldn't share His lot if he didn't get washed, Peter urgently exclaimed, "Then, please—not just my feet but my hands and my face as well!"

In spite of his rebellion, he had a sincere heart. Peter had no intention of breaking away from the Lord, and the possibility alarmed him. As usual, he didn't see himself as he ought to. So, just to make sure he would retain his part with Christ, he requested an entire bath if that was what the Lord required. Peter may have been stubborn, but his inner heart was honest. Thankfully God judges us by our heart attitude.

Scripture is filled with examples of such people. King David made many mistakes and sinned greatly. He committed tremendous sins. He committed adultery with one of his soldier's wives, then had the soldier killed to cover up for the baby who was coming. Yet, God says about David, "I have found David son of Jesse a man after my own heart" (Acts 13:22, NIV). Why? Because people look on the outward appearance, but God looks on the heart.

God can handle our temptations and failures if we are willing to continue trusting Him. God knows the failings of His saints because no one has ever lived who was not sorely tempted by something. Even Jesus was tempted, but He never sinned.

I have met people who claim they don't have a problem with temptation. Hogwash! Either they are covering something up, or they are so out of touch with Christ that they don't recognize their need.

I also have met people who resent discussing problems with sexual temptations. These people sometimes feel that once we become Christians we don't have a problem with that. Such people are deluded or kidding or completely different than I am. All the way through life, from youth to old age, a normal person is continually tempted.

I remember becoming acquainted with an eighty-five-year-old doctor, a missionary in Argentina, who was a distinguished man of God. I was seventeen and very impressed with him.

One day he came to our home, as he did once in a while, and took me into the living room alone to talk with me. I was experiencing all the normal struggles and temptations of an adolescent and fervently longed for the day when I would be godly enough not to be troubled by them.

In those days, I thought only young people were tempted sexually. I figured the moment you married, temptation was gone. Many people still think that. This doctor seemed so righteous and pure to me that I was stunned when, in the course of our conversation, he honestly admitted to still being tempted sexually.

That talk opened my eyes. Christians constantly face temptation, but the Lord has provided help for us through His indwelling presence.

THE FOURTH OBSTACLE
Not Accepting the Warnings of Scripture

Pat has a friend—I'll call her Carol—whose husband recently left her for another woman. Pat knew

Carol was hurt, devastated. Pat felt her friend might be tempted, first, to take revenge on her husband and, second, to play around with another man to show her husband that she's still got it. So Pat wrote Carol a letter—straightforward, to the point, but in a loving way—even though she wondered if Carol would ever speak to her again.

Some time later, we visited Carol and she pulled out Pat's letter. "I have been tempted in both areas," she said, "so I carry the letter in my wallet."

That's something, isn't it? Carol accepted the letter from my wife as a warning from God. Because she heeded this warning, God protected her from making what would have surely been a disastrous mistake.

The Lord graciously warns us through His Word and through other believers. Scripture repeatedly warns believers about the obstacles and problems of the Christian life and gives us guidelines on how to handle ourselves. We are told to be especially cautious when we feel most confident because that is when we are most likely to be caught off guard. Unless we accept the warnings, however, we are candidates for failure.

Let's take a look at Peter, who ultimately ignored the warning Jesus gave him in John 13:36–37.

> Simon Peter said to him, "Lord, where are you going?"
>
> "I am going," replied Jesus, "where you cannot follow me now, though you will follow me later."
>
> "Lord, why can't I follow you now?" said Peter. "I would lay down my life for you!"

"Would you lay down your life for me?" replied Jesus. "Believe me, you will disown me three times before the cock crows!"

In Luke 22:31–34 Peter again ignores an important warning.

"Oh, Simon, Simon, do you know that Satan has asked to have you all to sift like wheat?—But I have prayed for you that you may not lose your faith. Yes, when you have turned back to me, you must strengthen these brothers of yours."

Peter said to him, "Lord, I am ready to go to prison, or even to die with you!"

"I tell you, Peter," returned Jesus, "before the cock crows today you will deny three times that you know me!"

In spite of Christ telling Peter that Satan wanted to trouble him, Peter wouldn't take the warning seriously. He still didn't know himself. He sincerely believed he was ready to go to prison and to death for Christ. He insisted that even if all the other disciples denied Christ, he would remain faithful. Peter didn't realize that the threat from Satan was real.

Know Satan Is Real

Why is it that a good Christian man suddenly runs off with some young woman? Why does he abandon his wife and children, and bring bitterness, agony, loneliness, and destruction into his life and his family's?

We have talked to many men and women who have failed in this area and they say, "I don't know what happened. If I had to do it over again, I would never have made that decision."

All of us have been tempted to do things that, in the end, hurt us, our spouses, our children. Why is this? The explanation is simple. It is Satan. The Bible strongly cautions us about our enemy.

Scripture warns us that Satan is a real enemy, not just a story to frighten children. He isn't a figment of our imaginations, created to keep bad people in line. Satan is alive and active.

Look around you. Has Satan sifted families around you? Has he disrupted your own family?

We live dangerously close to disaster when we don't take seriously Scripture's warnings about the power of Satan and our need to trust Christ's indwelling power day by day, moment by moment. If you think you can ignore the warnings of Scripture and avoid Satan's influence, you are taking a dangerous chance. The most dedicated and disciplined people sometimes are the very ones who fall flat. Just look at the rash of Christian leaders who have slipped into sin in recent years.

Ephesians 6:10–20 tells us to prepare ahead so we will be able to stand in the evil day. It tells us we will be attacked by Satan and encounter evil days, but we can remain strong because we are prepared, armed with God's Word.

To the prepared Christian, Satan's attacks are futile. The believer stands on the promises of the indwelling Jesus Christ, and that is sufficient.

Use Spiritual Weapons

Carnal weapons are another obstacle to maturity Christians must face.

I remember giving God an ultimatum as a young man. I wanted to win souls to Christ, but felt I didn't have the gift of evangelism. No matter how hard I tried, no one was coming to faith in Jesus Christ.

I gave God a deadline: "If I don't see any converts by the end of the year, I'm quitting." I would be an active Christian, but I planned to simply teach other believers.

The end of the year came and went. No converts. Now I was sure I didn't have the gift of evangelism.

Four days into the new year, I attended a home Bible study. The speaker never showed up, so I was recruited. I was completely unprepared. However, I had been reading a book based on the Beatitudes. So I read Matthew 5:1–12 and repeated whatever I remembered from the book.

As I was commenting on the beatitude, "Blessed are the pure in heart, for they will see God" (NIV) a lady suddenly stood up. She began to cry: "My heart is not pure. How can I see God? Somebody tell me how I can get a pure heart."

I don't remember the woman's name, but I will never forget her words: "Somebody tell me how I can get a pure heart." Before the evening was over, that woman found peace with God and went home with a pure heart overflowing with joy.

I had tried my hardest, used all my talents, but to no avail. Only when I quit using carnal weapons, when I gave up and let God work through me, did I see any results.

In Luke 22:35–38, Jesus teaches His disciples this principle. He says,

> "That time when I sent you out without any purse or wallet or shoes—did you find you needed anything?"
>
> "No, not a thing," they replied.
>
> "But now," Jesus continued, "if you have a purse or wallet, take it with you, and if you have no sword, sell your coat and buy one! for I tell you that this Scripture must be fulfilled in me—'And he was reckoned with transgressors.' So comes the end of what they wrote about me."
>
> The disciples said, "Lord, look, here are two swords."
>
> And Jesus returned, "That is enough."

Then in John 18:10–11 we are told that while the soldiers were taking the Lord Jesus prisoner, "Simon Peter, who had a sword, drew it and slashed at the High Priest's servant, cutting off his right ear. (The servant's name was Malchus.) But Jesus said to Peter, 'Put your sword back into its sheath. Am I not to drink the cup the Father has given me?'"

The Lord seems to have set Peter up for this one. Until now, all the crises between Peter and the Lord Jesus had been of Peter's own making. When Jesus said buy a sword, Peter, in zealous obedience, happily got a sword.

Perhaps he thought that now he could show everyone, including Christ, how faithful he was and how much he loved Jesus. Perhaps he felt he could, with his actions in defense of Christ, redeem his past errors. Whatever Peter's motivation, his dramatic attack resulted only in cutting off one fellow's ear.

Peter probably expected the Lord Jesus to commend him for his faithfulness. Instead he was told to put his sword away, while Jesus repaired the damage.

It seems everything Peter did brought reproofs, warnings, rebukes, and criticism by Christ. But he must have been completely shocked by this event. His Lord was about to be crucified and Jesus called it "My Father's cup." Peter could not understand why he shouldn't defend his Lord in the face of death.

Then Jesus explained, "I could call for a hundred thousand angels and they could defend me." Dear Peter, with all his zeal, was not needed. Compared to Christ's weapon of power, Peter's weapon was nothing.

When we are desperate and not walking in the indwelling power of Jesus Christ, we all have the tendency to begin to use carnal weapons of our own making. We may rely on something we studied in college, some book we just finished reading, or something we heard someone say. Instead of trusting the power of almighty God who has come to dwell within us through the resurrected Christ, we gather together ineffectual swords and hack away under our own power.

But in spiritual warfare, only spiritual weapons will do. Paul tells us even though we live in the flesh, we don't operate after the flesh. "The weapons we fight with are not the weapons of the world. On the contrary, they have divine power to demolish strongholds. We demolish arguments and every pretension that sets itself up against the knowledge of God, and we take captive every thought to make it obedient to Christ" (2 Cor. 10:4–5, NIV).

Show God's Power

While planning for a crusade in Costa Rica, we thought everything was going to go fantastically. When we got to Costa Rica, however, we discovered that certain leaders in the country suddenly had turned against mass evangelism. They had spread the word during the month of preparation that mass evangelism didn't produce any results, that it was old-fashioned, that all this saving of souls was unimportant compared to the great social issues of our day.

Some of the theologians—well-known and respected Christian leaders—insisted that this crusade was old-fashioned and that leading people to Christ would do nothing for the country. They decided they were not going to waste their time or money on a crusade to bring people to Christ.

I had to kneel day after day during the first week of the four-week crusade and say to the Lord, "Thank You for bringing us here. We know You are in control of this crusade. We don't want to take control ourselves. We want to show Your power."

I was greatly tempted to use carnal weapons and verbally blast our attackers from the pulpit. Controlling this temptation was difficult for me, but my team and I knew the Lord could show His power and relevance in the world much better than we could. Our faith brought thrilling results.

Many new believers got involved in churches; we received many, many letters from decision makers. The Christian radio station in that town received thousands of phone calls demanding that the crusade sermons be replayed every morning. Some people even put ads in the newspaper asking the station to play those messages every evening. The evangelistic messages ended up being broadcast on radio for three months, twice a day, at public request.

We never suggested to people that they contact the radio station. They did it on their own. As a result, Costa Ricans knew the gospel had power to change people's lives. But God, not we, moved the people to overcome the obstacles.

When you feel tempted to use carnal weapons, recognize your attitude as an obstacle to maturity. Say, "No, Lord. It would feel good to do _____. But, Lord, I know it would be wrong. It would dishonor You, and I want *Your* power to use Your weapons."

Surrender Your Will

After Christ rebuked Peter for drawing his sword, the Bible tells us that Christ was led away and Peter followed. Peter had not yet experienced the lowest point of his life, the final blow.

> Then they arrested him and marched him off to the High Priest's house. Peter followed at a distance, and sat down among some people who had lighted a fire in the middle of the courtyard and were sitting round it. A maidservant saw him sitting there in the firelight, peered into his face and said, "This man was with him too."

But he denied it and said, "I don't know him, girl!"

A few minutes later someone else noticed Peter, and said, "You're one of these men too." But Peter said, "Man, I am not!"

Then about an hour later someone else insisted, "I am convinced this fellow was with him. Why, he is a Galilean!"

"Man," returned Peter, "I don't know what you're talking about." And immediately, while he was still speaking, the cock crew. The Lord turned his head and looked straight at Peter, into whose mind flashed the words that the Lord had said to him. . . . "You will disown me three times before the cock crows today." And he went outside and wept bitterly (Luke 22:54–62).

Peter made a critical error by defending himself, by covering up his association with Jesus. In John 12:24–25 Jesus said, "I tell you the truth, unless a kernel of wheat falls to the ground and dies, it remains only a single seed. But if it dies, it produces many seeds. The man who loves his life will lose it, while the man who hates his life in this world will keep it for eternal life" (NIV).

Thousands of Christian men and women are useless to the cause of Christ. They belong to Christ, but are not overflowing with Christ because they're trying to save their own lives. They are always protecting themselves, always covering for themselves, always justifying themselves, always explaining why they can't do this or that. We must be willing to give up our will for His, our lives for His life through us. That is taking up the cross.

In this final crisis Peter failed totally and irrevocably. Peter, who only a few hours before had promised to go to jail and even die for Christ if necessary, denied he ever even knew the Man. Peter found it so important to remove himself from all associations with Jesus that he denied knowing his Master with oaths and curses to a lowly maid whose opinions really posed no real danger for him.

It is painful to see Peter pushed all the way to total and unnecessary denial. Certainly God didn't want that. The Lord doesn't want us to suffer the logical consequences of our weaknesses. He would rather we turn them over to Him long before they get us into critical difficulties.

A woman told me of a tragedy she experienced. "My husband and I ministered to children. We were dedicated to Christ and had won many children to the Lord. Our dedication was a source of self-pride, self-satisfaction. But we had to be brought to our senses. You know what did it? The death of our baby. When that happened, we realized how enchanted with ourselves we were. When we lost our child, we realized our work was a privilege for God. Serving Him, being alive, being a Christian, and winning children for Christ was a blessed responsibility. Our lives have really been filled with the Spirit since that time."

Does God want us to endure all that pain? I don't think so. But often we bring pain upon ourselves when we refuse to go the way He asks us to go.

The Lord loves us. He is very patient and gracious. But we can't play games with God. Eventually, if we resist His guidance and disregard His will, He is going to let us go all the way in our willful direction, whatever it happens to be. For some it may be immorality, for others a life-sapping drug habit or alcohol addiction, for still others an emotional breakdown. The stakes are high when dealing with eternal values.

A very touching incident occurred when the Lord looked at Peter. The Lord, surrounded by His accusers, saw Peter deny Him. And when the cock crowed, the Lord Jesus took time to look at Peter. Christ didn't speak or even make any signal. He just looked at him. It must have been quite a look because the Bible says Peter went out and wept bitterly. Jesus said volumes to Peter in that look, and, for a heartbroken Peter, all Christ's words and warnings fell into place. What months of teaching had failed to do, a quiet look accomplished in a moment.

Suddenly Peter saw himself. He saw it all and was repentant. Imagine this sensitive man, crushed, walking alone through the hills of Jerusalem wrenched and weeping. His Lord had been taken, the disciples scattered, and he was alone with his terrible guilt and his Master's words echoing in his head.

It is fortunate in some ways that Scripture does not record the details of Peter's pain, for few people in history have suffered so terrible a conclusion to such great anticipation.

Chapter 6

EXIT SIMON, ENTER PETER

Jim, a vice president of a large corporation in Oklahoma, was diagnosed three years ago with melanoma cancer. He underwent surgery twice, but the cancer returned, worse than before.

Jim told me, "Until recently, I had fought all my battles and thought I could continue to do so. Right after the third tumor was discovered, I began to realize that help was needed, but I wasn't sure where to look or what to look for."

Jim heard about our crusade in Tulsa and attended the business/professional luncheon. This, he said, was the beginning of the journey back to God for both him and his wife, Marcia.

The next evening, Jim and Marcia came to the Tulsa Convention Center for the nightly crusade meeting and both recommitted their lives to the Lord. "When we arrived earlier that evening," he said, "we were two. When we left, we were three: The Lord, Marcia, and Jim. What a team!"

What does God want from us, really? What is His goal as He tests our faith, permits great obstacles to hinder our growth, and allows defeat and pain to overwhelm us? He wants to bring us into a relationship with Him. He wants to change us from relying on ourselves to relying on Him. He wants to make us powerful and godly Christian men and women.

I believe that's what Peter gained from his sometimes thrilling, but often agonizing, experience of knowing Jesus.

In John 21:1–19 we read about Peter's next encounter with Jesus, who had already been crucified, had risen from the grave, and had been witnessed by some of the disciples. If Peter has been changed Scripture will certainly record it.

Later on, Jesus showed himself again to his disciples on the shore of Lake Tiberias, and he did it in this way. Simon Peter, Thomas (called the twin), Nathanael from Cana of Galilee, the sons of Zebedee and two other disciples were together, when Simon Peter said, "I'm going fishing."

"All right," they replied, "we'll go with you."

So they went out and got into the boat and during the night caught nothing at all. But just as dawn began to break, Jesus stood there on the beach, although the disciples had no idea that it was Jesus.

"Have you caught anything, lads?" Jesus called out to them.

"No," they replied.

"Throw the net on the right side of the boat," said Jesus, "and you'll have a catch."

So they threw out the net and found that they were now not strong enough to pull it in because it was so full of fish! At this, the disciple that Jesus loved said to Peter, "It is the Lord!"

Hearing this, Peter slipped on his clothes, for he had been naked, and plunged into the sea. The other disciples followed in the boat, for they were only about a hundred yards from the shore, dragging in the net full of fish. When they had landed, they saw that a charcoal fire was burning, with a fish placed on it, and some bread. Jesus said to them, "Bring me some of the fish you've just caught."

So Simon Peter got into the boat and hauled the net ashore full of large fish, one hundred and fifty-three altogether. But in spite of the large number the net was not torn.

Then Jesus said to them, "Come and have your breakfast."

None of the disciples dared to ask him who he was; they knew it was the Lord.

Jesus went and took the bread and gave it to them and gave them all fish as well. This is already the third time that Jesus showed himself to his disciples after his resurrection from the dead.

When they had finished breakfast Jesus said to Simon Peter, "Simon, son of John, do you love me more than these others?"

"Yes, Lord," he replied, "you know that I am your friend."

"Then feed my lambs," returned Jesus. Then he said for the second time, "Simon, son of John, do you love me?"

"Yes, Lord," returned Peter. "You know that I am your friend."

"Then care for my sheep," replied Jesus. Then for the third time, Jesus spoke to him and said, "Simon, son of John, *are* you my friend?"

Peter was deeply hurt because Jesus' third question to him was "Are you my friend?" and he said: "Lord, you know everything. You know that I am your friend!"

"Then feed my sheep," Jesus said to him. "I tell you truly, Peter, that when you were younger, you used to dress yourself and go where you liked, but when you are an old man, you are going to stretch out your hands and someone else will dress you and take you where you do not want to go." (He said this to show the kind of death by which Peter was going to honor God.)

Then Jesus said to him, "You must follow me."

God is not trying to make us religious. He is not trying to make us toe the line. He is not trying to make us dedicated, bitter, tense, self-sufficient people. Not at all. He is trying to bring us into a relationship with Him where we are controlled by Him. He wants us to be happy, joyful, free, fruitful—real men and women of God.

He does not expect us to be perfect, but He does expect us to learn control. He does not expect sinlessness, but He does expect maturity. And He does not expect us to do this alone. He has begun the work in us, and He has promised He will finish it.

Controlled at Last

My wife and I know a woman who, when she was a young widow, had an affair. The man, who promised to marry her, told her he was divorced when he wasn't. She became pregnant and had a little boy. Because she felt so ashamed and guilty, this woman even stopped going to church and moved from her small town to a bigger city in another state. One day, this repentant woman decided she needed to attend church again. So every Sunday she sat in the very back of a small church and, throughout the entire service, would weep tears of repentance.

Several of the elders noticed her behavior and, after finding out what she had done, told her: "You are obviously repentant. God has forgiven you. You don't have to feel guilty. Let us restore you into the fellowship of the church because you're forgiven!" And, as a restored Christian, this woman began being used by God to lead scores of people to Himself.

If you have wandered away from the Lord, if in a moment of weakness or in a time of rebellion you have messed up your Christian life, don't give up on yourself and on God. The Lord says to you, "Don't stay away from Me. I will have mercy on you. Although I cannot heal some of the things you've done, it will keep you broken and humble for Me the rest of your days. But I will restore you, and I'll give you opportunities to serve Me."

When we humbly recognize our failures and truly repent, God will continue to use us. Look at Peter. God continued to work with Peter until his dying day, and He accomplished great things through him.

When Jesus Christ called and commissioned Peter again, Peter must have experienced great confusion. His denial had been so severe, his cursing and swearing so out of order that he must have felt Christ was through with him. He had, in fact, returned to his old business of fishing. But it wasn't all over for Peter in spite of what he may have felt and what he had done.

Many Christians believe at one time or another that what they did last week, or last month, or ten years ago, was so bad they do not deserve to have anything more to do with the Lord. Some people, when overwhelmed by guilt, believe they have sinned against the Holy Spirit and have no more hope. But when a Christian experiences such deep concern, it proves that the living God is still at work in his or her life. God is calling the believer to Himself.

Christ appeared to Peter after His resurrection (1 Cor. 15:5). After He had risen from the grave, the Lord Jesus went looking for Peter. Jesus, more than anyone else, knew how Peter had suffered at the cross, so He looked for him first after His resurrection.

Then the Lord allowed Peter to become a fisherman again so He could remind Peter of his original calling.

When Jesus met Peter the first time, the situation was identical. They were fishing, they had caught nothing, the Lord stepped into their lives, and everything was changed. When Peter once again discovered the barrenness of self-effort, the Lord showed up. Jesus then gave Peter a promise even better than the first one.

Jesus asked Peter, "Simon, son of John, do you love me more than these others?" He used the Greek word *agape,* meaning divine love—that perfect sacrificial love only God can give us. When Peter replied, "Yes, Lord, you know that I am your friend," Peter didn't use *agape.* He used *phileo,* which means friend.

The Lord was asking Peter if he loved Him with that perfect love he had vowed when making a commitment to go to prison or die for Christ. Peter could only admit to a great affection, a friendship for Christ.

A second time, Jesus asked if Peter loved Him with a divine love, and a second time Peter could only admit to friendship.

The third time, Jesus asked his question differently. "Simon, son of John, are you my friend?" Jesus met Peter at his own level when He asked, "You claim to feel great affection and friendship toward Me. Can I rely on that claim? Do you really mean, this time, what you are saying to Me?"

No wonder Peter was deeply hurt. With Christ's last question he recalled the pain and grief he had felt at betraying his Lord after promising sacrificial— *agape*—love. Peter, who finally had learned his lesson and seen himself so accurately, realized he was incapable of promising anything beyond friendship.

He had found a new honesty. He no longer pretended to give what he had not found the strength to give. Pretense was gone; arrogance was gone. No longer did he dare to suggest he knew more than the Lord. For the first time, Peter responded honestly, "Lord, you know everything. You know that I am your friend!"

Christ changed His question for him. He did not demand more of Peter than Peter could give. But Peter was, in fact, giving all that Christ desires from a believer—an honest, contrite, and humble heart.

Once he was honest enough to confess that he didn't even trust his own love toward the Lord, then the Lord said to him, "Peter, feed my lambs, tend my lambs, feed my sheep." Christ gave Peter a new commission.

Empowered by the Holy Spirit

Not only was Peter called back and recommissioned, he was also empowered by the Holy Spirit and sent out as a leader of the budding church (see Acts 2). All previous commissions were promises Peter couldn't fulfill. He had to mature first; he had to grow into his commission.

The Lord had promised Peter he would grow to be so different that he would be a rock, and the Lord always keeps His promises. It wasn't until Pentecost, however, that the promise began to come true. When the Holy Spirit formed the real church (the body of Christ indwelt by the Holy Spirit), Peter began to become the kind of man Jesus had in mind when He met him years before by Caesarea and called him to be a fisher of men.

How far along have you come in your Christian walk? How many months or years have passed since Jesus Christ took over in your life? How much of the old ways have begun to be relegated to the past and how much of the new maturity has been coming to the fore?

How much of the Peter side of you can your spouse see in your home? How much of the Peter side can your children see as you talk and function in the family? In the church, are you a Simon or a Peter? Are you a loud, opinionated, self-sufficient church member? Or are you a fruitful, gracious, Christ-controlled individual. Have you learned to see yourself as Christ sees you?

Have you grown to maturity in Christ, whatever your age? There is a difference between growing up and just growing older. Many people have grown old but have never grown up. Have you grown up in Jesus Christ? Can you honestly say, "I have a long way to go. I'm not where I will be, but by God's grace I'm not where I was. Bless God, I'm with Him!"

Maturity doesn't mean we're perfect. When Peter received the fullness of the Spirit at Pentecost, he was not perfect, but he was controlled. He was not sinless, but he was growing and maturing and he did so for the rest of his days.

That should be the goal of every Christian. Isn't that where we want to be? We can't expect perfection this side of heaven. The Lord Himself said He has to work with each one of us until the day He returns. We will never be perfect until the day of Jesus Christ, but we should be controlled by the indwelling Christ and growing daily.

So dynamic was Peter's life that even today it glorifies God whenever we read about him. Study his epistles, examine his life, and you see a weak man who came face to face with Jesus Christ and is still bearing fruit two thousand years after his death.

My son Stephen used to ask me, "Dad, are you a legend in your own time?" With a chuckle I'd reply, "You'd better believe it."

Although my son's comment was somewhat humorous, as Christians we all can be "legends" in our time. God promises a great legacy to those who live godly and righteous lives. Psalm 112 tells us, "Blessed is the man who fears the LORD, who finds great delight in his commands . . . . His righteousness endures forever; his horn will be lifted high in honor" (verses 1, 9, NIV).

If the Lord doesn't return in this generation and we die, wouldn't it be great if years from now people would learn something of Jesus Christ through our lives?

Saint Augustine was such a person. Although born in A.D. 354, his life still speaks to believers. We study his words, written so long ago, and see a man who lived under the control of Christ in spite of weaknesses.

God used Martin Luther, born in 1483, to change the history of the Christian church. Today, nearly five hundred years after his death, God still speaks to believers through his example of courage and conviction.

John Calvin, George Whitefield, the Wesleys, and Hudson Taylor were buried years ago, but God still speaks to Christians through their commitment.

Many other quiet people have lived in such a way that their lives still speak God's message and blessing and promises today. What will your life show twenty years or one hundred years or five hundred years from now? How will people remember your life?

Jesus Christ's purpose in dealing with Peter was not to squelch him and crush him. Jesus desired to make Simon Peter one of the greatest people in all history. The point was to get Peter out of the way and let Christ take control of his life. Although Peter was not perfect, from the day of Pentecost, the savor, the flavor, the perfume of Jesus Christ exuded from his life. We can still smell His perfume as we study Peter's life today.

Paul said in Galatians 2:20, "I have been crucified with Christ and I no longer live, but Christ lives in me. The life I live in the body, I live by faith in the Son of God, who loved me and gave himself for me" (NIV).

When I discovered that simple secret, my whole life was transformed. How I thank God for the men God used to put His hand on my life until it hurt. The pain of seeing myself as God sees me made me realize that it was not what I was going to do for God, but what Christ was going to do through me that counted.

Chapter 7

THE PETER PROMISE

"He knew so much about the Bible; he had such a great ministry. How could this happen to him?" People often have asked me such questions when a Christian leader has fallen because of money, sex, or pride.

The unasked question is left hanging in the air: "Since this happened to such a spiritual man (or woman), am I going to fall too?"

I used to answer, "We're all vulnerable. It could happen to anyone," echoing what other Christians have said in the past.

Some time ago I knew a middle-aged man in South America who was one of the most winsome evangelists I have ever heard. But he had an attitude toward money that was unholy. He put away money that wasn't his. Now he is no longer an evangelist. He is doing something else when he ought to be winning souls in the harvest field of Latin America.

A respected American youth evangelist with whom I had worked in the past left his wife, his children, and his ministry for the passions of the flesh. It turned out that secretly, for years, he had been feeding a pornography addiction while railing against immorality. Then, the inevitable happened. He started committing adultery. He had affairs going in city after city. Finally, the truth came out, and he walked out on his family.

When the truth was revealed, I was shaken. It seemed to only prove the point: "We're all susceptible to moral failure, right?"

I'm not so sure anymore. I now believe such thinking leads to fatalism, smacks of false humility, and flies in the face of Scripture.

Failure Is Not Inevitable

"We're all vulnerable" isn't true—if we're staying in God's Word, if we're walking by the Spirit, if we're obeying Jesus Christ. "If you do these things," 2 Peter 1:10 says, "you will never fall" (NIV).

Peter isn't using flowery language; he isn't simply trying to make us feel better. These words are from the Bible; God Himself tells us, "If you do these things, you will never fall." What a wonderful promise!

Earlier in the same chapter Peter tells us, "His divine power has given us everything we need for life and godliness through our knowledge of him who called us by his own glory and goodness" (2 Peter 1:3, NIV).

"All power" has been given to us through Jesus Christ, and His power is what enables each of us to live a godly life.

God doesn't want us to shipwreck our faith, shatter our homes, disgrace our churches, or destroy the ministries He has entrusted to us. Instead, He has given us His indwelling presence and designed the Christian life so that we'll succeed.

Walls of Protection

To keep us safe in His hand, God has established several strong walls of protection around us: the Word of God, including His moral laws; the body of Christ, especially our local churches; and His indwelling Holy Spirit, who is ever sensitive to sin in our lives.

But we can't just sit around hoping God will protect us when temptation comes our way. As John Wesley recognized during the Great Awakening, it is as Christians grow in grace and go on to maturity that they will be kept from falling. "Paradoxically," Wesley biographer A. Skevington Wood reminds us, "to stand still is to be in danger of slipping back" (NIV).

I encourage you to take action. First, don't gossip and gloat when someone goes ahead and flagrantly sins. We dare not secretly get a kick out of seeing someone else fail. Since temptations are common to us all, Scripture calls us to walk humbly in the fear of the Lord.

Second, make a radical decision to be holy as God is holy. Pray to God about your area of weakness. I did this early on in my ministry. I told God, point by point, how I behave in certain situations. I was embarrassed and recognized that God already knew how I acted, but it did me good to tell Him. Then I took Galatians 2:20 and reaffirmed with God my resolution to be crucified with Christ. I made a radical decision to be holy under every circumstance, without exception.

Third, begin an accountability group with a few of your Christian friends. Let them know about your area of weakness—you don't have to share in great detail. Ask them to hold you up in prayer before God as well as to hold you responsible for your actions. I meet each Wednesday with a group of respected, godly leaders in my city and have discovered great benefits.

Fourth, get back to reading the Bible. Several years ago when a rash of leaders were falling one after another, I asked my mentor, Dick Hillis, founder of one of the world's leading missions organizations, "Why are all these guys falling away?"

Dr. Hillis thought and thought about my question. After walking with the Lord for over sixty years, he's no fly-by-night. Finally, he told me, "I think it's because they were reading a lot of books about the Bible, but not the Bible itself."

The more I thought about it, the more I could see his point. Nothing can take the place of God's Word, not even the best biblical commentaries. Sure, an evangelist or preacher or teacher needs to do his homework. He needs to read widely and deeply. But we need to saturate ourselves with God's Word so, as the psalmist wrote, "I might not sin against [God]" (Ps. 119:11, NIV).

As we read the Bible, associate with godly men and women, and follow the Holy Spirit's leading, we are protected and kept safe in God's hand.

Beware of Temptation

That's not to say we won't be tempted to climb over these divine walls of protection. For this reason we must beware of several seemingly innocent mistakes that make us vulnerable to Satan's attacks: carelessness and opportunity, overconfidence and self-reliance.

Maybe we begin to hurry through our daily Bible reading or prayer since we really don't have much time. Perhaps we place ourselves in tempting situations. Maybe we're trying to serve God in our own power instead of in the power of the Spirit. It could be we're feeling proud after gaining a victory over temptation. However it happens, carelessness creeps in and that's when Satan strikes. The opportunity arises, and we fall into sin.

Overconfidence and self-reliance also cause us to stumble. We forget to daily bear the cross and think that perhaps Christianity is not as difficult as the Bible suggests.

Have you ever gotten up in the morning and determined you were going to be a nice person all day long? "I'm going to be pure today," you say to yourself. "I'm not going to have impure thoughts. I'm not going to get angry. I'm not going to covet. I'm going to be holy today." What happens?

Within an hour you fail. You see your neighbor heading out with his boat and wish you had the money to be able to skip work like he does. You start yelling at that driver who cut you off on the freeway. You see something that begins a stream of lustful thoughts. Self-confidence and self-reliance won't keep us from falling and are a poor substitute for daily walking with God and relying on His indwelling power.

But we don't have to fall into that trap. The Bible promises, "God is faithful; he will not let you be tempted beyond what you can bear. But when you are tempted, he will also provide a way out so that you can stand up under it" (1 Cor. 10:13, NIV). We are not helpless victims of Satan's whims. He can defeat us only if we let him. Remember the Peter Promise: "If you do these things, you will never fall."

Resisting Temptation

We have three recourses when we are tempted. First we can take comfort in *the mind of Christ*. God tells us in 1 Corinthians 2:16 that the mind of Christ is now ours. If by faith we appropriate His indwelling presence, we can keep our thinking straight. It doesn't eliminate the temptation, but it helps us keep our thinking consistent with what Christ wills.

Second, *the indwelling power of the Holy Spirit* helps us implement the thinking of the mind of Christ. On our own we will surely fall. But when we rely on the indwelling power of the Holy Spirit, we can overcome.

A friend of mine has often said, "Woe to the person who has to learn principles at a time of crisis." That is good advice. We must learn to rely on Jesus Christ before a crisis strikes so we know how to stand firm.

One day I was in the airport and watched as some teenagers said goodbye to one of their friends. One of the teens told her departing friend, "Good luck, Mary." Mary took hold of a rabbit's foot she was wearing around her neck, began rubbing it, and said to her friend, "With this, how can I have anything but good luck?"

Mary felt she was prepared for anything because she wore a rabbit's foot around her neck. It's silly, but Christians often rely on a spiritual rabbit's foot to protect them from Satan. They think going to church or carrying a Bible will keep them safe from attacks by the Evil One.

Third, we need *the right kind of input*. The Bible says in Philippians 4:8–9, "Finally, brothers, whatever is true, whatever is noble, whatever is right, whatever is pure, whatever is lovely, whatever is admirable—if anything is excellent or praiseworthy—think about such things. Whatever you have learned or received or heard from me, or seen in me—put it into practice. And the God of peace will be with you" (NIV). What we entertain in our minds affects the whole personality.

Temptation never goes away, not even for the holiest of men and women. But we have the power to overcome impurity of mind and misdirected passions through the indwelling power of the Holy Spirit.

The Lord doesn't want us to panic, to be fearful that we'll be the next to fall. He "is able to keep you from falling and to present you before his glorious presence without fault and with great joy" (Jude 24, NIV).

Let's not go around cringing anxiously, frightened we're going to fall. We don't need to be afraid of the world, scared that our sexuality, or whatever, is going to destroy us. If we are walking and growing in Christ, the Scripture says we will never fall—and that's a promise!

When Christ Takes Over

The Christ who made Peter the great apostle he was is the same Christ who lives in you and me. He can make us into the men and women He wants us to be when we give Him control of our lives. All He asks is to take over. And when He takes over, it's amazing what He can do through us.

Peter's life raises important issues for each Christian who is struggling to follow Christ. Where are you in the light of God's promises and God's purposes for you? Is God still dealing with you, or have you resisted His voice so long and run so far away that you can't hear it anymore? Have you returned to fishing while the Lord calls you from the shore? If so, dive into the water, swim quickly to Jesus, and listen to His renewed call and commission. When you go to Him, you will be able to say, "The life I live in the body, I live by faith in the Son of God, who loved me and gave himself for me" (Gal. 2:20, NIV).

CORRESPONDENCE

If this book has motivated you to let Jesus Christ take over in your life, or if you have been helped in any other way through the varied ministries of the Luis Palau Evangelistic Association, please let me know. My address is:

> Luis Palau
> P.O. Box 1173
> Portland, OR 97207
> USA

RECOMMENDED READING

To further enrich your Christian life, look for the following books in your local Christian bookstore. If the store doesn't have one of these books in stock, ask the clerk to order it for you.

Authentic Christianity by Ray C. Stedman (Discovery House Publishers)

Body Life by Ray C. Stedman (Discovery House Publishers)

Designed To Be Like Him by J. Dwight Pentecost (Discovery House Publishers)

God's Loving Word: Exploring the Gospel of John by Ray C. Stedman (Discovery House Publishers)

Healthy Habits for Spiritual Growth by Luis Palau (Discovery House Publishers)

The Priority of Knowing God by Peter V. Deison (Discovery House Publishers)

Say Yes! by Luis Palau (Discovery House Publishers)

Where Do I Go From Here? by Dave Branon (Discovery House Publishers)

ABOUT THE AUTHOR

Who is Luis Palau? Perhaps you've followed his ministry with interest for years. Or perhaps this book is you first introduction to the man.

Luis Palau is now becoming well known in his adopted homeland, America. His popularity in Latin America, the United Kingdom, and other parts of the world is rather remarkable.

During one crusade, more than 528,000 people in London turned out to hear Luis Palau in person. And a crowd of 700,000 people gathered to hear Luis on Thanksgiving Sunday in Guatemala a few years ago.

In many ways, Luis stands out in this generation as a truly international Christian spokesman and leader. He's a third generation transplanted European who grew up in the province of Buenos Aires, Argentina, and then chose to become an American citizen after completing the graduate course at Multnomah Biblical Seminary in Portland, Oregon.

Equally at ease in English and Spanish, Luis Palau's solidly biblical, practical messages hit home in the minds and hearts of listeners around the world.

"Luis is probably more in demand among evangelicals to preach and speak than almost any other person in the world," says Billy Graham. "Wherever there is an evangelical conference they try to get Luis Palau, because he is a powerful preacher. But more than that, he is an evangelist to whom God has given a multiplicity of gifts."

Luis Palau has proclaimed the Good News of Jesus Christ to hundreds of millions of people via radio and television in ninety-five countries, and face-to-face to more than eleven million people on six continents.

The impact? Many thousands of people have trusted Jesus Christ and become established as disciples in local churches. Cities and nations have heard a clear proclamation of the gospel. Luis Palau's burden is to see the same thing happen in America, in this generation.

Luis and his wife, Pat, also a popular conference speaker and author, have served as missionary-evangelists in Costa Rica, Colombia, and Mexico. The Palaus have four grown sons and now make their home in Portland, Oregon, near the international headquarters of the Luis Palau Evangelistic Association.

Note to the Reader

The publisher invites you to share your response to the message of this book by writing Discovery House Publishers, Box 3566, Grand Rapids, MI 49501, USA. For information about other Discovery House books, music, or videos, contact us at the same address or call 1-800-653-8333. Find us on the Internet at http://www.dhp.org/ or send E-mail to books@dhp.org.